Generis
PUBLISHING

Circassia in the World History

Hamed Kazemzadeh

Copyright © 2024 Hamed Kazemzadeh
Copyright © 2024 Generis Publishing

All rights reserved. This book or any portion thereof may not be reproduced or used in any manner whatsoever without the written permission of the publisher except for the use of brief quotations in a book review.

Title: Circassia in the World History

ISBN: 979-8-88676-284-6

Author: Hamed Kazemzadeh

Cover image: www.pixabay.com

Publisher: Generis Publishing
Online orders: www.generis-publishing.com
Contact email: info@generis-publishing.com

Table of Contents

1 CHAPTER - HUMAN GEOGRAPHY & ETHNOGRAPHY 7

Introduction 7

Circassia – Homeland 9
    Etymology 11
    Geographical Landscape 12
    Geographical Distribution 14

Circassian People 16
    Tribes 17
    Identity 18
    Beliefs 25
    Language & Literature 30

Ethno-Political Issues 32

2 CHAPTER - HISTORICAL BACKGROUND 35

Introduction 35

Rise up in the History 36

Circassia in 18th-19th Centuries 41

Russo–Ottoman War 43
    Belgrade Treaty (1739) 44
    Küçük Kaynarca Treaty (1774) 45
    Jassy Treaty (1792) 46
    Bucharest Treaty (1812) 47
    Adrianople Treaty (1829) 48
    Crimean War (1853 - 1856) & Paris Treaty (1856) 49

Caucasian War 49
    Murid War 52
    Caucasian Military Line 53

Russo - Circassian War 54
    Kabardian Role 57
    Consequences of Russian Conquest 58

British Connection..61

MAPS 69

FIGURES 83

BIBLIOGRAPHY 93

1 Chapter - Human Geography & Ethnography

Introduction

The Circassian[1] is a generic noun that refers to the people of the Northwest Caucasus as an ethnic group. Their human geography and ethnography thence are important to be reviewed that has been highlighted over the past five hundred years in the history of the Caucasus, and it can be a preliminary study to answer the *Circassian Question* and also identify the most important issues relevant to the *Circassian Question*. Ethnographically, the Circassians is known by themselves as '*Adyghe*'[2] who are native to the land, which is named *Circassia*[3]. They originally inhabited the area of the Northwest Caucasus, though after the Russian conquest of 1864 almost fully half of them immigrated to the Ottoman Empire's territory. Nowadays, those Circassians who stayed in Russia mostly have spread in three republics of *Adyghea*[4], *Kabardin-Balkar*[5], *Karachay-Cherkess*[6] as well as two Krais[7] of *Krasnodar*[8] and *Stavropol*[9] under the *North Caucasian Federal District*[10] in the Russian Federation. Religiously, most of them currently are *Sunni* Muslim of *Hanafi* School[11] and much more than other Caucasian Muslims are depend on the mosque and regional *Mufti*[12], so I can call their *'Muslimness'* is mosque-centered faith.

The Circassians speak the *Circassian Language*, which is a Northwest Caucasian language that is called *Abkhazo-Adyghean*[13]. The Circassian language itself is divided into two official dialects that include the literary languages of *Adyghean* and *Kabardian*[14]. Western and Lower dialect often called the *Adyghean*, and an Eastern and Upper one, the *Kabardian* (Jaimoukha, 2001: p. 245). The first Circassian written were modified *Perso-Arabic* script, then the *Latin* was adopted, and finally, in the late 1930s, the *Cyrillic* was used under the

---

1. Pronunciation: in UK: /sɜrkæsi.ən/, in US: /sərkæsən/, in Russian: Черкесы *Cherkesi*,
2. In Circassian: Адыгэхэр *Adygekher*, in Russian: Адыги *Adigi*
3. In Circassian: Адыгэ Хэку *Adige kheku*, in Russian: Черкéсия *Cherkesia*, in Georgian: ჩერქეზეთი *Cherkezeti*, in Arabic: شيركاسيا *Shirkasia*, in Turkish: *Çerkesya Cherkeisa*
4. In Russian: Респýблика Адыгéя *Respublika Adigeya*
5. In Russian: Кабардúно-Балкáрская Респýблика *Kabardino-Balkarskaya Respublika*
6. In Russian: Карачáево-Черкéсская Респýблика *Karachayevo-Cherkesskaya Respublika*
7. A krai or kray in Russian: край, was a sort of geographical administrative division in the Russian Empire and in the Russian SFSR. It is also one of the types of the federal subjects of current Russia.
8. In Russian: Краснодáрский край *Krasnodarsky kray*
9. In Russian: Ставрополь́ский край *Stavropolsky kray*
10. In Russian: Сéверо-Кавкáзский федерáльный óкруг *Severo-Kavkazsky federalny okrug*
11. In Arabic: حنفي *Hanafi*, is one of the four religious Sunni Islamic schools of jurisprudence.
12. In Arabic: مفتي *Mufti* is an Islamic scholar who interprets and expounds Islamic law.
13. It called also *Circassic*, or sometimes *Pontic*.
14. In Russian: Кабардинцы *Kabardintsi*

Soviet era. Currently efforts are underway to devise a new Latin-based script among the young generation and some elites to get understandable and readable for every Circassian, specifically for Diasporas who do not know Russian (Ibid: p. 254).

The Circassian people consists the twelve tribal communities in their human geography: *Abzakh, Besleney, Bzhedugh, Hatuqwai, Kabardian, Mamkhegh, Natukhai, Shapsug, Temirgoy, Ubykh, Yegeruqwai,* and *Zhaney* that the names of dialects also directly come from their tribe name (Gammer, 2004: p. 67). I should mention that the current Circassian flag where each star on the green and gold means one of their tribes (Figure. 01). However, in the 20th century, the Circassians were designated as the following: *Adygheans, Cherkessians, Kabardians,* and *Shapsugians* under Soviet Union administrative divisions, although all the four are essentially the same people as we called them 'Circassians'.

Almost 800,000 Circassians remained in Circassia and the Russian Federation. According to the 2010 Russian Census recorded 718,727 Circassians registered including 516,826 are *Kabardians*, 124,835 are other *Adygheans*, 73,184 are *Cherkessians*, and 3,882 *Shapsugians*[15] (Census, 2013) (Table. 01). Among diaspora, it is estimated about 2 - 4 million populations mostly in Turkey, Syria, Jordan, and Egypt (Mullen & Atticus, 1997: pp. 67-69) (Table. 02).

Racially, they are comprised of European type race in the anthropology. In fact, based on Encyclopedia of World Cultures by David Levinson a lot of them have blue eyes and blond or light hair, whereas others have dark hair with light complexions. Some groups show a propensity toward long, aquiline faces and dolichocephalic heads, whereas others tend toward round faces (Colarusso, 1994) (Figure. 02). However, the Circassians are a mountain people with strongly hierarchical social structure and aristocratic tradition, famed within the Caucasus and beyond for personal beauty and martial skills (Kosven, 1961: pp. 142-57). Unfortunately, little is known of their origins and early history, because lack of the written texts. Besides, the European travelers noted that the Mountaineers did not have their own writing system. In recent years, the Circassian communities around the world tried to manage their identity and survival subjects, also worrying about their future. Re-engaging and recalling their past with all its honorable and painful details requires the necessity to follow-up effects that show how to find a solution to the *Circassian Question* with identifying the perpetrators and selecting the appropriate mechanism of applying the related rules for the realization and recognition of their legal rights.

---

15. In Russian: шапсуги *Shapsugi*, Turkish: Şapsığlar *Shapsiqlar*

In this chapter, I try to identify these people and land based on ethnography methodology according to the primary and secondary sources, which are available Online, and in libraries. Therefore, I focused on three parts, first the territory of historical homeland of Circassians, second I will go for introducing this person as an ethnic and a nation and then finally I will survey the ethnopolitical issues in the North Caucasus regarding Circassians' activities.

Circassia – Homeland

The historical homeland of the Circassians by themselves called *'Xekwzch'* that means *'Old Country'* where in all sources in English used Circassia (Chisholm, 1911: pp. 380-381). The land of Circassia pronounces and names in different format in each languages of the region, for example in in Russian: *Cherkesia*, in Georgian: *Cherkezeti*, in Arabic: *Shirkasia*, in Turkish: *Cherkesia*, and in Persian: *Cherkesestan* that is referred to the region in the Northwest Caucasus and along the Northeast coast of the Black Sea. According to the Greek sources, another historical name was used for this land and its people as *Zyghoy*, who were described by *Strabo*[16] as a nation and country in the north of Colchis[17]. The first mention of the name 'Circassia' was made by *John de Plano Carpini*[18], the representative or envoy of *Pope Innocent IV*[19] to the Great Khan of the Mongols in 1245 AD (Avezac, 1839: p.776) (Table. 03).

It is very difficult to visualize the borders of Circassia today, despite limited geographic resources and contradictory contents. This point should consider that there never was a union state in this territory, and only the tribes with a complex social structure managed the country. Nevertheless, it is possible to delineate historical Circassia, a term used to designate *Adyghean* lands before the commencement of the *Russian-Caucasian War*[20] at the end of the 18th century. Geographically, I can summarize the historical Circassia where extended from the coastal area of Black Sea at the entry of the Azov Sea, thence over the Caucasian Range and southeastward along its eastern downhills into the

---

16. Strabo in Greek: Στράβων Strábōn; (63 BC - 24 AD) was a Greek geographer, philosopher, and historian who lived in Asia Minor during the transitional period of the Roman Republic into the Roman Empire.
17. Colchis in Georgian: კოლხეთი *Kolkheti*; in Greek Κολχίς *Kolkhis* was an ancient kingdom and region on the coast of the Black Sea, located in present-day in the west of Georgia.
18. Giovanni da Pian del Carpine in English as John of Pian de Carpine, John of Plano Carpini or Joannes de Plano (1185 – 1252 AD)
19. Pope Innocent IV in Latin: Innocentius IV (1195 - 1254), born Sinibaldo Fieschi, was Pope of the Catholic Church from 25 June 1243 to his death in 1254.
20. Russian-Caucasian War in Russian: Кавказская война *Kavkazskaya vojna* was from 1817 to 1864 as an invasion of the Caucasus by the Imperial Russian Army.

weathering of the *Baksan*[21], *Malka*[22], and *Kuma*[23] rivers, then into the Kabardian plain in the north of the Terek River[24], thereupon northwestward to the path of the Kuban[25], and along the south bank of the Kuban back to the Taman Peninsula[26] (Colarusso, 1994) (Map. 01).

This original homeland was bounded on the west by the Black Sea; on the northwest by the Crimea; on the north by Ukraine; on the east by the territory of the Chechens and Daghestanis; to the south by Ossetian, and Georgian highlands; and to the southwest by Abkhazian land[27]. The area engirded was more than 100,000 sq. km, almost a quarter of the size of the Caucasus. Additionally, there are some historical maps of Circassia which made in the 19th century, can help to visualize their territory (Map. 02).

In this land, homogeneous peoples, such as Circassians, Abazins[28] and Abkhazians, lived together with heterogeneous ethnic groups such as Ossetians[29], Balkars[30], Karachays[31], Tatars[32] and Cossacks[33]. In addition, Sochi[34] is considered by many Circassians as their historical capital city (Economist, 2012) (Map. 03).

---

21. In Russian: река Баксан *Reka Baksan,* also known as Azau River (Length: 173 km) mostly located in the Republic of Kabardino-Balkaria which flows east-northeast and joins the Malka River.
22. In Russian: река Малка *Reka Malka,* also known as Balyksu River (Length: 210 km) mostly located in the Republic of Kabardino-Balkaria, which forms the northwest part of the Terek River basin.
23. In Russian: река Кума *Reka Kuma,* a major river (Length: 802 km) in the Northern Caucasus, flows through Southern Russia into the Caspian Sea, mostly located in in the Republic of Karachay-Cherkess.
24. In Russian: река Терек *Reka Terek,* a major river (Length: 623 km) in the Northern Caucasus, flows through Georgia and Southern Russia into the Caspian Sea, mostly located in the Republic of North Ossetia.
25. In Russian: река Кубань *Reka Kuban,* a major river (Length: 660 km) in the Northern Caucasus, flows through Southern Russia into the Black Sea, mostly located in the Krasnodar Krai.
26. In Russian: Таманский полуостров, *Tamanskiy poluostrov,* a peninsula in the present-day in Krasnodar Krai, borders on the north with the Azov Sea, on the west with the Strait of Kerch and on the south with the Black Sea.
27. In Russian: Абхазы *Abkhazi* are a Northwest Caucasian ethnic group, mainly living in Abkhazia and a disputed region on the Black Sea coast.
28. Abazin or Abazinians in Russian: Абазины *Abazini,* are an ethnic group of the Northwest Caucasus, closely related to the Abkhaz and Circassian people.
29. Ossetians or Ossetes in Russian: Осетины *Osetini,* are an Iranian ethnic group of the Caucasus Mountains.
30. Balkars in Russian: Балкарцы *Balkartsi,* are a Turkic people of the North Caucasus.
31. In Russian: Карачаевцы *Karachavetsi,* are a Turkic people of the North Caucasus.
32. In Russian: татары *Tatari,* are a Turkic people living mainly among Slavic people who was applied to a variety of Turco-Mongol and semi-nomadic states. More recently, the term refers mostly to the people who speak one of the Turkic languages among Slavic communities.
33. In Russian: казаки *kazaki,* are a group of East Slavic-speaking people who are mostly living in Southern Russia and in South-Eastern Ukraine.
34. In Russian: Сочи *Sotchi* is a city in Krasnodar Krai, located on the Northeast of Black Sea coast near the border of Georgia/Abkhazia.

Etymology

As I mentioned above the Circassians refer to themselves as *Adyghe*[35]. It should be noted the self-designation of a group of people is the first term, whereas outsiders to refer to them specifically from their neighbors use the second. The name of *Adyghe*, according to Edmund Spencer[36] who traveled through Circassia in the 19th century, is from *Atté* in Circassian language means 'height' to signify a mountaineer or a highlander person, and *Ghéi* which means 'sea' that totally we can translate and signify 'a group of people settlement and inhabiting in the mountainous land near the sea coast' (Spencer, 2008: p. 06, 164). In this regard, *Loui Loewe* who collected the Dictionary of the Circassian Language in 1854 had the same opinion about entomology of *Adyghean* word (Loewe, 1854: p. 05).

However, the name of Circassian has occasionally applied to *Adyghe* as well as *Abaza* in the historical texts (Latham, 1862: p. 279). Actually, it represents a Latinization of *Siraces*, the Greek name for the north of *Colchis*, as well as called *Shirkess* by Khazars and later used *Cherkess*, as the Turkic name for the *Adyghea*, and originated in the 15th century with medieval *Genoese* merchants and travelers to Circassia. (Latham, 1859: p. 50) On the other hand, folk etymology explains the name of *Cherkess* as a meaning of 'warrior cutter' or 'soldier cutter', from the Turkic words of *çeri* that means soldier and *kesmek* that means cut (Klaproth, 1814: p. 558; Taitbout, 1837: p. 05). In Turkey, *Cherkess* name is used in reference to all descendants of the people who came from the North Caucasus in the 19th century as *Muhajer*[37], even including Ossetians and Chechens (Atham, 1859: p. 50).

Nevertheless, there is another opinion that Circassian name derives from the name of the earlier people, *Kerkets* which we can find in some Arabic, Persian, Georgian and Armenian sources (Lavrov, 1956: p. 40). For example, the famous Muslim traveler, *Al-Massoudi*[38], visited the Northwest Caucasus in the 10th century and described the Circassians, whom he referred to as *Kashak* or *Keshek*. In the middle ages, the Russians used to refer to them by the name *Kasogi*, later *Kossogh*, which is related to Old Georgian *Kashaqi* and Old Armenian *Gashk*. The Ossetians still call them *Kasag*, so we can conclude that

---

35. Also as Adige, Adyga, Adyge Adygei, Adyghe, Attéghéi and in Circassian: *Адыгэ Adygè*, in Russian: *Адыгu Adigi*
36. Captain Edmund Spencer was a prolific British travel writer of the mid-nineteenth century. Name of his book: Travels in the Western Caucasus, in 1836
37. *Muhajer* مهاجر is an Arabic word that means immigrant.
38. Or Al-Mas'udi in Arabic: أبو الحسن علي بن الحسين بن علي المسعودي *Abu al-hasan Alī ibn al-husayn ibn Alī al-Masūdī*; (896–956) was a Muslim historian and geographer from Baghdad.

the name of Circassia was referred to as *Kasaxia* in Byzantine Greek texts (Jaimoukha, 2001: p. 11).

Despite a common self-designation, Russians took the name of *Cherkess* for all Circassians before the Soviet Union. However, later and based on new geographical and political divisions, they called them separately *Kabardian, Cherkessian, Shapsugian* and *Adyghean*. In Persian, however, the word is applied generally to peoples living beyond Derbent city in Dagestan and all over the North Caucasus (Minorsky, 1943: p. 163). Even by referrals to 'The History of Mubarak Ghazani' written by *Rashid al-Din Faḍlullah Hamadani*[39] in the 13th Century, *Cherkess* means four[40] tribes or four *Keshek* (Faḍlullāh Hamadānī, 2016: p. 134).

The native self-designation was first recorded in the fifth century BC. It was explained as a corruption of an older term *Antixe*, the *Ants* being people thought to be ancestral to Adyghe, and *-xe* the plural suffix. The *n* was elided, the *t* transformed to *d*, and *x* turned into a soft *g*. It is perhaps related to the old name *Zyghoy*, which Strabo used to designate the Circassians. *Zixi* or *Zyghoy* was the Latin and Greek appellation, which was first recorded in the fourth century AD by Roman historians and travelers. So based on this theory, we can say on the contrary of the previous opinion, the name of *Cherkess* can be a Turkic corruption of the Greek name of *Kerxetai*, or it may mean 'Bandit'. It was recorded in 1551 AD by *Giorgio Interiano*[41], one of the principal historians of the Genoese period (Jaimoukha, 2001: p. 12).

Circassia and the *Circassians* nouns used to evoke many romantic notions of beauty, bravery, and courage in western literature. However, different names in different periods, even the proximity of some names, as well as abundant names in small geography, have made the inaccuracy of the original names and history of many Caucasian peoples in a hint of ambiguity (Table. 04).

Geographical Landscape

Geopolitically, Circassia is located in Eastern Europe and geographically, in the Northwest Caucasus near the northeastern Black Sea coast. It almost covers the entire fertile plateau and the steppe of the northwestern region of the Caucasus (Map. 04).

---

39. Also known as Rashīd al-Dīn Faḍlullāh Hamadānī in Persian: رشیدالدین فضل‌الله همدانی, (1247–1318) was a public official, historian and physician in Ilkhanate-ruled of Persia.
40. *Chehar* in Persian
41. He (15th century) was a Genovese traveler, historian and ethnographer. His travelogue "La vita: & sito de Zichi, chiamiti ciarcassi: historia notabile" was among the first sources of the life and customs of the Circassias.

In eastern Circassia, where precipitation ranges between 600-720 mm per annum, forests are interspersed with mountain pasture and steppe. The average annual temperature in *Kabardin-Balkar* is about 10 degrees. Near *Nalchik*[42], the climate is continental and toward the south, as far as the forests on the foothills the climate is moderate. Just a little higher up the mountains, the climate is harsh and sharply divided, with hot summers and cold winters (Jaimukha, 2001: p. 27).

In the western Circassia, annual rainfall reaches 3.500 mm, under the influences of the moist climate of the Black Sea basin. On the coastal plains, the climate is warm and humid, growing cooler as the Caucasian foothills are crossed. There are many water flows, rivers, and runnels throughout the region, many of which run through fully forested flumes.

The main feature of the Circassia is the mountain ranges, which extend from the Northwest to the Southeast. The southern slopes are more precipitous and their terrain is rougher than the northern ones. The highest and most impressive being the middle of Circassia, which includes *Elbrus*[43] (Figure. 03). Elbrus in Circassian language is called *Waschhemaxwe* that means 'happy mount' and it is a holy mount for locals and Circassians.

The western mountain stretches from the eastern *Anapa* in the extreme northwest of *Circassia* to *Gagra* in Northern Abkhazia. It runs almost in parallel with the shore for about 360 km, generally increasing in height, before it turns inwards in an easterly direction. The narrow coastal strip is mostly rugged terrain. There are three systems associated with the main rivers *Terek, Kuma*, and *Kuban*. The former originates in the middle of the Caucasus in the territory of the *Kabardin-Balkar Republic* and ends at the Caspian. It is fed by five main rivers, the *Cherek*[44], *Chegem, Baksan, Kurkuzhin, Malka*, and a multitude of lesser ones. The *Kuban*, which is one of the largest rivers in the Caucasus, belongs to the *Pontine River* system. Historically it formed the boundary between Eastern and Western Circassia. It also has its sources in the middle of the Caucasus, but it follows a northwesterly direction and its delta is on the Azov Sea (Map. 05).

In summary, geographical landscape of Circassia includes three important items, which were influenced on their identity and history. First, one is the Western Caucasus Mountain and specifically *Elbrus*, which was their refuge and shelter during struggles with others. Therefore, many of the Circassian folklore

---

42. Nalchik in Russian: *Нальчик,* is the capital city of the Kabardino-Balkaria Republic
43. Mount Elbrus in Russian: Эльбрýс *Elbrus*, is the highest mountain in Europe with 5.643m. A dormant volcano, Elbrus is in the Caucasus Mountains in Southern Russia, near the border with Georgia.
44. In Russian: река Черек *Reka Cherek,* (Length: 76 km) mostly located in the Republic of Kabardino-Balkaria which is a right tributary of the Baksan River and Terek basin.

and mythological stories have taken place around this mount. The second one is rivers that I mentioned above specifically *Terek, Kuma* and *Kuban*. Based on archeological excavations the most of ancient civilizations of Circassia and North Caucasus were located around these rivers. The last one in my point of view is coastal plains where they could build their contemporary history and the Sea could survive them. Even their historical capital Sochi is situated in this part.

Geographical Distribution

Under domination of imperial Russian and the Soviet Union rule, ethnic and tribal divisions between the most of the peoples were increased, terminating in several different actuarial names being used for various parts of the *Circassian People* who includes *Adygheans, Cherkessians, Kabardians, Shapsugians*. Consequently, there is an effort among Circassians to unite under the name Circassian in Russian Censuses to reflect and revive the concept of the Circassian nation.

The majority of their Diaspora already tends to call itself Circassian. The Circassian diaspora refers to the resettlement of the Circassian population, especially during the late 19th and early 20th centuries. From 1763 to 1864, the Circassians fought against the Russian Empire in the *Russo-Circassian War*[45], finally succumbing to a scorched-earth campaign initiated in 1862 under *General Nicholai Yevdokimov*. Subsequently, huge numbers of Circassians were exiled and displaced to the Ottoman Empire and other nearby areas; others were moved and resettled in imperial Russia far from their homeland.

Therefore, when we want to talk about geographical distribution, we have to focus just on the Circassia not on other lands of their Diaspora. Later in the 4th chapter, we will back to diaspora and their distribution, but just as a quick mention, the majority of Circassians live outside of the Russian Federation, where their exact numbers are impossible to determine. The following estimates have been made by the Caucasus Trust (CT) and the Federation of the Caucasus Associations (KAFFED): Turkey: 1,000,000 - 7,000,000; Jordan: 20,000-100,000; Syria: 100,000 (ORSAM, 2012: p.4); Israel: 15,000 (Gammer, 2004: p. 64); and other countries: 500,000 (KAFFED, 2005) (Table. 02).

---

45. The Russo-Circassian War (1763–1864) refers to a series of battles and wars in Circassia, the northwestern part of the Caucasus, which were part of the Russian Empire's conquest of the Caucasus lasting approximately 101 years, starting under the reign of Tsar Peter the Great and being completed in 1864.

The division of their distribution into the Russian Federation is as follows: 1. The Kabardin-Balkarian Republic, 2. The Karachai-Cherkess Republic, 3. The Adyghea Republic, 4. The Shapsug Region (Map. 06).

The Kabardin-Balkar is a federated republic where is located in the *Terek River* basin. According to the census of 2010, about 859,939 populations (Census, 2013) include *Kabardians* 57.2%, *Russians* 22.5% and *Balkars* 12.7% as residing in the Republic (Howard, 2012: p. 310). Its capital is Nalchik and the head of the republic is *Yury Kokov*[46].

The *Karachay-Cherkess* first was established as an autonomous oblast in 1923 and transformed to the republic in 1993 where is located in the upper Terek basin. According to the 2010 Census, *Karachays* make up 41% of the republic's population, followed by *Russians* 32%, *Cherkessians* and *Abazins* together make up 20% (Ibid: pp. 299-308). Cherkessk[47] city is the largest city and the capital of the *Karachay-Cherkess* Republic. This republic has five official languages such as *Cherkess, Russian, Karachay-Balkar, Abaza,* and *Nogai*. Currently, *Rashid Temrezov*[48] is the Head of the republic.

The Republic of *Adyghea* is situated inside the *Krasnodar Kray* and lying in the plain and valley of the *Kuban River*, which is populated mostly by Russian ethnicity. It is population of 439,996 included 64.5% *Russians*, 24.2% *Adygheans*, and 3.4% *Armenians* (Ibid: p.346). *Maykop*[49] is its capital city and the current Head of republic is *Murat Kumpilov*[50].

Currently, all these republics administratively are part of the *North Caucasian Federal District*. The last region is not officially registered nowadays and called the *Shapsug*. The name is one of the twelve tribes of the Circassian people and historically, the *Shapsug* tribe used to make up one of the biggest groups of Circassians and controlled the ports of *Dzhubga*[51] and *Tuapse*[52] to mountain Gorges (Richmond, 2008: p. 22).

On 6 September 1924, the *Bolsheviks* established the *Shapsug National Region*[53] as a part of the Black Sea Region. The center of the whole district was

---

46. In Russian: *Коков Юрий Александрович*, is a Kabardian politician who is the head of Kabardino-Balkaria since 2013.
47. Cherkessk in Russian: *Черкесск*, is the capital city of the Karachay-Cherkess Republic.
48. In Russian: *Рашид Бориспиевич Темрезов*, is a Karchayian politician who is the head of Karachay–Cherkessia since 2011.
49. Maykop in Russian: *Майкоп*, is the capital city of the Republic of Adyghea and located on the right bank of the Belaya River.
50. In Russian: *Мурат Каральбиевич Кумпилов*, is an Adyghean politician who is serving as the head of the Republic of Adyghe since 2017.
51. In Russian: *Джубга*, is a seaside resort situated 57 km west of Tuapse in Krasnodar Krai.
52. In Russian: *Tyance*, is a town in Krasnodar Krai, Russia, situated on the northeast shore of the Black Sea, south of Gelendzhik and north of Sochi.
53. The Shapsug National District or Shapsug National Rayon in Russian: Шапсугский национальный район *Šapsugskij nacional'nyj rajon,* was a district that was established in 1924 as a national district for the Circassian Shapsugs tribe of the Black Sea within the Krasnodar Krai.

the city of *Tuapse* in the coast of Black Sea. After the end of the Second World War in 1945, the Shapsug National region was renamed *Lazarevsky District*. The *Shapsug* called it *Psyşwap* instead of *Lazarevsky*, because *Lazarevsky* was named for *Mikhail Lazarev*[54] who facilitated the invasion and conquest of Circassia, and put a siege over it during the *Russo-Circassian War*. Nowadays this district is one of four city districts of the *Sochi* in *Krasnodar Krai*. In addition, the most of population is Russians and almost 3,000 *Shapougians* or generally, Circassians live in, but it is still a part of their distribution. Different sources note that before the Russo-Circassian War the number of *Shapsug* people was ranging from 150,000 to 300,000 (sochi, 2014). In all four regions, the Circassians form a rural village population, with the cities being predominantly Slavic peoples.

Circassian People

Generally, as it is mentioned above the Circassian people are the Caucasian ethnic groups from the Northwest Caucasus who call themselves as *Adyghean* in the simplest form and the Circassian word is usually used as a synonym for the *Adyghean People* in English (Shami, 1998: pp. 617-646). A slightly wider understanding suggests Circassian refers to the *Adyghean* and their ethnic kin, the linguistically extinct *Ubykh*[55] and the *Abkhaz-Abaza groups*. In its widest version, the Circassian is used to refer to all the North-Caucasian Diasporas including the East Caucasian language speakers *Chechens*, *Ossetians*, or even *Turkic languages* speakers like *Karachay* or *Nogais*[56], etc (Kaya, 2004: pp. 221-239).

However, I have decided to use the English form of the name of these people. Therefore, the term Circassians denotes all or part of the indigenous peoples of the Caucasus who live in the Northwest Caucasus Range, the formidable chain that divides Caucasia into the *Transcaucasia*[57] to the south and Ciscaucasia[58]. There is no certain agreement as to whom exactly of those nations the appellation refers to. It is this last sense that is assumed in this thesis, and the terms *Adyghe* and Circassian will be used interchangeably.

---

54. Admiral Mikhail Petrovich Lazarev in Russian: *Михаил Петрович Лазарев*, (1788 - 1851) was a Russian fleet commander and an explorer.
55. In Circassian: пэху, туахы, убых; in Russian: убыхи; used to be one of the twelve Circassian tribes.
56. The Nogais in Russian: *Ногайцы* or *ногаи*, are a Turkic ethnic group who live in the North Caucasus. They speak the Nogai language and are descendants of various Mongolic and Turkic tribes who formed the Nogai Horde.
57. In Russian: Закавказье *Zakavkaze*, or the South Caucasus.
58. Ciscaucasia is the northern part of the Caucasus region.

It should be noted that this region is an important stronghold for them and the power struggle to control the region has been an important issue. Therefore, frontiers between varied indigenous tribes and familial groups have remained obscure and endlessly changing. The Circassians, together with the genetically and linguistically related *Abkhazians*, *Abazins* and the nearly extinct community of *Ubykh*, made up the indigenous population of the Northwest Caucasus. However, their languages were not mutually intelligible. The *Adygheans* was by far the largest nation of the Northwest Caucasus before their exile to Ottoman lands, and composed of many tribes: in the eastern part Kabardians and Beslanays; in the western part *Abzakh, Shapsug, Bzhedugh, Nartkhuaj, Kemirgoi,* and *Hatuqwey*. The *Shapsug* as I mentioned above also had their ethnic area within the borders of the Krasnodar Region until its abolition in 1945 (Jaimoukha, 2001: p. 95).

If I refer to historical texts, I should bring first the *Genovese Giorgio Interiano* definition of Circassians who left us in the 16th century just a brief description of the appearance of Circassians. He notes that the *Zixi* or *Zyghoy* was, par excellence, handsome and well-shaped, their beauty much admired among the *Mamluk Sultanate*[59] (Atalikov, 2010: p. 28). Nearly 300 years later, explanation of the anthropological look of Circassians got more accurate (Cherkasov & others, 2015: p. 75). Hence, for example, in narrating the appearance of a Circassian man, *Frédéric Dubois de Montpéreux*[60] notes: "The Circassian inhabiting the seashore is tall in stature, shapely in body and limbs, and thin in waist; relentless in striving to enhance this type of beauty, even more, he tightens his waist with a leather belt. His gait is graceful and light, his head is oval-shaped; by default, the *Mahometan*[61] shaves his head but keeps a mustache and grows a black non-thick beard; as black are his deep-set eyes; his not long thin nose is quite shapely; the frame of his jaw is elongated and clearly defined. Quite often you can come across Circassians with auburn hair and beards" (De Montpéreux, 2010: pp. 40-41).

Tribes

The Circassians generally were divided into tribes and clans especially when they want to identify themselves. They were made up of two groups: Eastern

---

59. *Mamluk Sultanate* was a medieval realm spanning Egypt, the Levant, and Hejaz. It lasted from the overthrow of the Ayyubid dynasty until the Ottoman conquest of Egypt in 1517. The Mamlūk state reached its height under Turkic rule with Arabic culture and then fell into a prolonged phase of decline under the Circassians.
60. He (1798 - 1850) was a Swiss travel writer, naturalist, archaeologist and historian. He is known for his travelogue toward the Caucasus.
61. Mohammedan (also spelled *Muhammadan, Mahommedan, Mahomedan* or *Mahometan*) is a term for a follower of the prophet of Islam "Muhammad".

and Western tribes. The *Kabardians*[62] and *Besleneys*[63] composed the Eastern branch; the most important Western *Adyghean* tribes can be listed as such: *Abadzekh*[64], *Temirgoy*[65], *Makhosh*[66], *Khatukhay*[67], *Natukhay*[68], *Shapsug*[69], and *Bzhedugh*[70] (Table. 05).

However, among them, just a few tribes have maintained a substantive presence in the Caucasus: *Kabardian, Beslanay, Temirgoi, Bzhedugh,* and *Shapsug*. The rest were exterminated, assimilated by other Circassian tribes or they already left to the Ottoman Empire in the 19th Century (Hewitt, 1999: p. 27).

It should be considered that Circassian tribes were divided into principalities, within which the rights and duties of individuals were ordained by a code of behavior called *Adige Xabze* or in English '*Circassian Etiquette*'. In this term, each person of Circassian society addresses based on his/her clan and tribe. Actually, this system of morals had evolved to ensure that strict martial discipline was maintained to defend the homeland against the invaders. Historically, in the 18th and the beginning of the 19th centuries, some Circassian tribes transformed to a more equitable system by overthrowing the ruling classes. However, these formed small clans and lived in secluded mountainous areas (Jaimoukha, 2001: p. 26).

Identity

As I mentioned above Circassian society had been tribal in structure, therefore the main identity of Circassian comes from their tribal background. While we want to talk about 'identity', we should define in advance. Actually, in the political science 'identity' plays a central role in work on nationalism and ethnic mentality (Horowitz, 1985; Deng, 1995). On the other hand, the idea of '*state identity*' is at the center of constructivist critiques of realism and analyses of state sovereignty in the international relations (Katzenstein, 1996; Biersteker & Weber, 1996), but generally 'identity' matter marks many arguments on gender, sexuality, nationality, ethnicity, language and culture (Young, 1990; Miller, 1995; Taylor, 1989) which I try to use this definition of 'identity' on this thesis

---

62. In Russian: *Кабардинцы Kabardintsi*
63. In Russian: *Бесленеевцы Beslenevtsi*
64. In Russian: *Абадзехи Abazekhi*
65. In Russian: *Темиргоевцы Temirgoevtsi*
66. In Russian: *Махошевцы Makhoshevtsi*
67. In Russian: *Хатукайцы Khatukaitsi*
68. In Russian: *Натухайцы Natukhaitsi*
69. In Russian: *Шапсуги Shapsugi*
70. In Russian: *Бжедуги Bezhedugi*

with focusing on linguistic and cultural matters. Even though here is the most relevant entry for 'identity' in the Oxford English Dictionary: "The sameness of a person or thing at all times or in all circumstances; the condition or fact that a person or thing is itself and not something else; individuality, personality"[71]. Note that this does not easily capture what we seem to mean when we refer to 'national identity' or 'ethnic identity', for example.

Regarding the ethnic and national identity, I should mention that it is a difficult concept to define. There are a lot of overlapping layers of self-conception, but there are by no means confined to, native language, religious faith, culture, history, and traditional homeland. In the post-Soviet era, discussions of ethnic and national identity have often brought out many political debates in the new emerging countries and nations. Afterward, identity in its willing incarnation has a twofold sensation. It refers at the same time to public categories and to the fount of an individual's self-esteem or serenity (Fearon, 1999: p.2).

Since the Caucasus invasion by Russian Tsar until the collapse of Soviet Union, due to the physical divisions of Circassia, I can say that the stabilization of national identity has never been practical. Even after the collapse of the Soviet Union, there have been no serious attempts at encouraging national and ethnic unity in the region by Circassian elites. However, this idea has never been implemented, due to various factors, including political pressures, geographical dispersion, and internal non-convergence.

Nevertheless, in my point of view, Circassian identity has found the unit meaning through their history that characterized by traditional and local economy, class system & social structure, customs & traditions, music & dance, religion & belief, language & literature and even their cuisine & traditional costumes which will be mentioned. Another item in the formation of Circassian identity is immigration and imagination, which are historical, linked processes that produce memorable moments in the pasts of peoples, nations, communities, and individuals. Therefore, in this case, Circassian diaspora has had long-term influences on their community, which is still observable among them. Diaspora identities are constructed in motion and along different lines than nation-states. Within a few decades, Circassian diaspora found themselves not Ottoman people but citizens of the new emerged states of Turkey, Syria, Jordan, Palestine, Israel and etc. The peak point in the historical processes of identity formation was the breakup of the Soviet Union and the free access to territories of the homeland, many of whom have now traveled to the Caucasus, some intending to settle permanently and it means that the identity still is shaping

---

71. 2nd edition, 1989

(Shami, 2000: pp. 178-181). In addition, the symbols that Circassians hold central to their sense of collective identity are derived from these historical experiences (Shami, 2009: p. 156).

Additionally, there was a discourse between officials in Russia and Diaspora regarding Circassian identity specifically before *Sochi Olympics*[72]. It is clear, though, that a patriotic sense of Circassian identity is emerging even despite a long history of exile, assimilation, linguistic and cultural change in different geographical distribution.

Traditional & Local Economy

The traditional economy is one of the most important parts of the Circassian identity, which was varied. The main traditional economy comes from breeding horses, cows, oxen, sheep, pigs, and chickens, and growing abundant fruits and vegetables. Apiculture in villages and the gathering of walnuts were also vital parts of their agricultural economy, as was hunting (Hotko, 2005: p. 416). The carpet weaving was a prime manufactured good that usually was based on women's housework. The Agriculture, craft industries, husbandry, and local manufacture were some of the activities of this class engaged in. Slaves could be released and freed in exchange for specific services. Peasants made up the infantry of a prince's army but were not allowed to don coats of arms (Wanderer, 1883: p. 05).

Despite the upheavals that have been rocking the Northern Caucasus since the fall of the Soviet Union, the Northwest Caucasus has escaped the worst and remains relatively peaceful and quiet. This is not to say that there are no tensions in the area. However, these are unlikely to result in serious armed conflicts and compromise the modest economic gains that have painstakingly been achieved in the past few years. Nevertheless, stereotypes are generally difficult to undo, and foreign investors are loath to inject their money into an area they perceive to be unstable. The transition to market economy has been fraught with difficulties and hardships. After more than seventy years of suppression of individuality and initiative, people found it difficult to adapt to new and unfamiliar conditions. In an effort to stimulate the economy and introduce the initiative, privatization was carried out on a large scale in the mid-1990s. However, it was those already in privileged positions who took advantage of the new opportunities and many became very rich, flaunting their newfound wealth. Ordinary people, on the other hand, saw their standards of living taking a nose-dive. Unemployment

---

72. The 2014 Winter Olympics officially called the XXII Olympic Winter Games.

soared and so did the concomitant crime and other ills resulting from social and economic imbalances and iniquities (Jaimoukha, 2001: pp. 123-128). Therefore, I can categorize their traditional economic on four groups, first of all, agriculture-apiculture, second transporting goods, third handy crafts and local arts, fourth trade on horse breeding, cattle trading and fishing.

Social Structure

The class system & social structure of Circassian society is the most important part of individual identity which each Circassian uses it for identifying themselves. This structure is complicated and is based on hierarchical feudalism. As it is mentioned above in feudal societies, laws preserved in the *ubiquitous*[73], which was differentiated according to class, regulated the rights and duties of each caste and defined class inter-relations. Quarrels and controversies were looked into by ad hoc councils whose jurisdiction ended after resolving the cases at hand. The feudal system almost ended in 1864 when Russia invaded and totally conquered Circassian lands. However, the institution was taken by the Circassians to the diaspora, where it survived for a few decades after in Ottoman territories. Towards the end of the 18th century, a series of upheavals rocked some parts of Western Circassia (Jaimoukha, 2001: pp. 156-158). According to *Paul B. Henze* in the book of 'Circassian Resistance to Russia': "After the Georgians and the Armenians, the Circassians came closest of all the Caucasian peoples to developing the prerequisites for nationhood. They had traditions of roots extending back to the dawn of recorded history" (Abtorkhanov, 1992: p. 67). Additionally, in the mid-16th century, according to the confirmation of the *Genovese G. Interiano*, the mountaineer groups were divided into nobles or aristocratic families, peasant and vassals, military serfs, and slaves. They did not tolerate their subordinates having horses like theirs. If someone outside the noble circle started to raise a foal, the nobles would take it away and give him or her a different animal in return, like a horned livestock animal. They would normally say to the person, "This is what's for you, not a horse" (Atalikov, 2010: p. 26).

Alongside of these historical notes, the Kabardians had the most intricate class structure among the Circassian tribes. At the top of the class, the structure is located Prince or *Pschi* then as his two hands *Tume* and *Mirze*. Under these two, there is *Werq*, which means the Nobility class. According to *Shora*

---

73. Xabze

Nogmov, the nobility was divided into five sub-classes, the commoners into four (Table. 06).

Amjad Jaimoukha has defined this structure accurately. He describes that each tribe was divided into princedoms, which were effectively independent, although there was a council of princes, which met at times of national crises. He says that "at the apex of each principality stood the prince who wielded almost absolute power over his subjects, who were considered as his property. The title of prince was hereditary, never acquired or bestowed. Although absolute power usually led to complete corruption, it was in the prince's interest to gain his vassals' unquestioned loyalty, which virtue was of the greatest essence in feudal society. Next to the principal caste came the nobles, who were divided into the proper and lesser nobility, and the vassals who were given a free hand in their fiefdoms in return for their allegiance" (Jaimoukha, 2001: pp. 157-160).

As it is much clearer now, this system was too complex, but the main point was its structure such as a pyramid that was based on the clans and tribes. In this structure, the age and richness of each person in society as well as was important. The Russian conquest and clump dismissal irrevocably undid the class system. Most of the higher classes who had moved to the Ottoman Empire before the end of the Russo-Circassian war, and they had sought to have their formerly subjects follow them to restore the class system in the new diasporic community.

Customs & Traditions

Traditional customs and social norms were enshrined in the orally transmitted rigid and complex rules named *'Adige Xabze'*[74] or 'Circassian Etiquette', which earlier was mentioned. The basic principle of Circassian customs and traditions should be sought through the *Xabze* that served as the law for ad hoc courts and councils set up to resolve contentious cases, other council issues and announce irrevocable judgments. Actually, *Adige Xabze* is complex rules for everyday life of a Circassian person that mostly are the unwritten traditional code of conduct that governed the Circassian communities across Circassia for centuries. It is included of Birth rules, Christening, Upbringing and Growing, Courtship and Marriage, Divorce and Bigamy, Disease and Treatment, Death and Obsequies, Greetings and Salutes, Generosity and Chivalry, Politeness and Respect, Blood-revenge, Hospitality, and Feasts.

---

74. In Russian: АДЫГЭ ХАБЗЭ *Adige Xabze*

Traditionally, the origins of the Etiquette are made reference to the golden era of the *Narts*, when its nucleus rules were provided. The characteristic of the *Narts*, as demonstrated in the oral tradition, were paragons that the Circassians through the ages had worked obstinately to imitate. It includes an obvious system of norms; behavioral rules and laws, which has been passed down from generation to generation, determines personal and community behavioral rules and is binding on all members of the community. The collective and individual attributes of these legendary heroes have shaped the code of behavior of Circassian society since time immemorial and molded the knightly characters of its nobility. These qualities included love of the homeland or fatherland and its defense to the last, idolization of honor, bravery and concomitant abhorrence of cowardice, observance of the code of chivalry, loathing for oppression, loyalty to clan and kin, fealty to bonds of camaraderie, care of and fidelity to one's horse (Jaimoukha, 2001: pp. 172).

In Circassian traditions could be found some rules which called *Adet*[75]. This collection of behavior signifies customary law as it prevailed. Its main tenets were hospitality, respect for elders, friendship behavior, blood-revenge, and chivalry. (Richmond, 2011: p. 214) It is sometimes used for, and confused with Xabze. In general, *Adet* referred to the law that regulated relations between the different peoples of the North Caucasus and it is a bit related to religious ethics, whereas *Xabze* was a specifically Circassian affair (Jaimoukha, 2009: pp. 4-8).

Therefore, I can summarize that from the cradle to the grave, the Circassian native creed[76], intertwined with the code of conduct, *Adige Xabze*, dictated the way an individual behaved in the society, formed his/her values and identity. The customs and traditions were the dual formers of the Circassian outlook on life and they meshed. Denying one of these nearly related components would have implicated releasing the other. Afterward, the mountaineers exhibited much permanence in the way of preserving their traditions. The conservatism of traditions was a distinctive trait of the Circassian life (Cherkasov & others, 2015: p. 83).

Music & Dance

The music and traditional dance of a nation or an ethnic is a reflection of its mores and psyche. This cultural phenomenon, which reflects the morale of the people of a land, is the best way to identify and verify the ethnic-national

---

75. In Russian: адэт *adet*, in Arabic: عادت *adat* is Arabic word that means custom or habit mostly back to Islamic ethic.
76. In Circassian: фIэщхъуныгъэ *Fieshkhunige*

identity. It is an illustration of its love for life graceful harmonic music fervors the feelings of man all over, and the Circassians, despite the imperfection of their local music, were charmed and cheered by it. Music was essential at celebrations as the accompaniment to dances and recitations of traditional poetries, and it revived up their dialogues.

The Circassian music has always been rich in dance tunes and melodies and reminds us the form of all Caucasian Dance, which is in general produced by an orchestra, as opposed to a single musician. The melodies for the songs and dances from the solo accordion players are a relatively recent orientation. Generally, dance music was played in *2/2 or 6/8* time with a background chorus (Adighe, 1956: p. 101).

Jaimoukha in his valuable work about the Circassian music says that "musical lore had been preserved by minstrels until the 1930s, by which time much of the music and songs had been collected and preserved. Some songs commemorate events that go back to the fourth century AD. Collection of music and songs started in the 19th century. However, systematic work only began in the Soviet period when many song collections were published. Books on the history of Circassian music were also issued, toeing the line of Communist historiography. Nevertheless, they remain seminal works indispensable in the study of Adygea [Adyghean] music" (Jaimoukha, 2001: p. 224).

In the Soviet era, this intricate history was molten into a more or less logical set of tales that maintained the specialty of each subgroup language families and identified collective dance as the most proper sense in which Pan-Caucasus commonalities should be valorized and demonstrated (Zhemukhov & King, 2013: p. 291).

Classical songs were generally executed in a singing sound, but without missing the beauty of a single syllable. It was nearly inconceivable to sing them without those sounds, which had given the songs harmonic forms and fetched rhyme into convenient melody. The Circassian music is characterized by certain instruments, including *Pshine*[77], *Pkhach'ach*[78], *Bereban*[79], *Pkhetaw*[80], *Apa-pshine*[81], *Qamlepsh*[82], and *Shik'epshine*[83] (Figure. 04).

Dance has a special position in the Circassian culture and their routine life. In mythical times, the *Narts* held annual festivals in which dances were held. None

---

77. An accordion which is played in a specific way to produce Circassian tunes
78. 2 sets of "wood blocks", each set containing about six pieces of wood held by hand; when a player strikes them together they produce a pure sound of wood to indicate the beat rhythm of the song.
79. A drum known as Dhol; in Adyghe it is called Shontrip. Struck by hand or two short batons. Drummers' hands bleed when they train, or overplay.
80. 'Wood-strike' made from wood looks like a small table and it is used for hitting it with sticks for tempo.
81. A three string lute
82. Circassian flute
83. A Circassian stringed instrument

of public or family gathering and festivity get complete without a round or more of dancing with singing. It kept the men dancers in utmost shape thanks to the energetic melody. Dance is originally a spiritual ritual, a kind of lively prayer in the Circassian culture. Afterward, it turned into a figure of lyrical celebration, remaining some of its ceremonial importance. All kind of dances in the region is based on the wealthy material of Circassian folklore (Figure. 05).

Generally, women's movements were graceful and reserved, no wild movements being required or displayed. The new descendant of female *sedate* dancers sometimes seizes the chance of informal séance to show off intense moves, in the parody of their male partners. In one modern comic choreography, gender-bending females perform acrobatic feats, strictly masculine affairs, with a flourish (Jaimoukha, 2010: p. 01).

As a result, the environment in which music is performed, the manner in which folk songs are performed, and the audience constitute the memory codes of cultural transmission. Music is the product of the common sentiments, ideas, philosophy, the way of social perception and interpretation of the society in which it is generated, and it is in this respect one of most powerful and functional channels of social communication. Hence, music and dance both generates a social identity of its own society and carries the characteristics of belonging to that particular geography and society in which it is produced.

Beliefs

As it is mentioned earlier, the religion of ethnicity must be important determinants of identity formation, therefore, the link between religion and identity will be reviewed among Circassians in Circassia and Diaspora. Actually, the religion is more likely to play the significant role in identity formation in a culture where ethnicity or a nation confront a continually fluctuating social and political milieu. Essentially, the transcendent meaning derived from religious affiliation is important for identity development and well-being. In the absence of the viewpoint available through religious beliefs, the worldview it provides, and its role in shaping and guiding behavior, the multiplicity of choices and options accessible to the modern community is more likely to breed despair, hopelessness, and confusion (Oppong, 2013: pp. 10-16). The religion can provide definitive answers and viewpoints about slippery issues of life that might be more fascinating and relevant for a generation and a nation who are trying to shape their identity, as well as the religion was a crucial component in the life of the mountaineering community (Erikson, 1964: p. 24).

The Circassian religious beliefs had been centered around a spine of *polytheism*, *animism*, and *paganism* with some *Christianity* and *Islamic* influences until the early part of the 19th century. It may be that the nature and the set ways of the Circassians played a significant part in impressing the indigence beliefs and sidelining spiritual imports. The *Monotheistic* faiths have had little suffering on the Circassian way of life in this environment and this explains the selector nature of the Circassian system of beliefs emphasized by outsiders. At the end of the Middle Ages, the Circassians were kept in the middle of a power struggle between Russian *Orthodox Christianity*, Ottoman *Sunni Islam*, and even Persian *Shi'a Islam*. They reverse their religious loyalty and allegiance very undoubtedly, converting from *Islam* into *Christianity* and vice versa, as the position demanded and for convenience (Minahan, 2000: p. 354). *Shi'a Islam* has never been into the Circassian religious identity; however, the Circassian slaves in Persia were converted to *Shi'ism* in the 16-18th centuries.

It should be noted that considering the '*Adige Xabze*' as the traditional religion of the Circassians is a common mistake made even by the Circassians. Whereas ancient religion regulated the spiritual and ritual domains, but the *Xabze* regulated the daily aspects of a Circassian's life. The substantive source of information on the Circassian beliefs and ritual ceremonies is the *Nart Epos* or *Nart Sagas*[84] (Jaimoukha, 2009: pp. 5-8) which will be explained further.

Pre-Islamic Beliefs

As regards, in other antique faiths, the genesis of the indigenous Circassian mechanism of beliefs is wrapped in suspicion and interlaced with myth and legend. The Circassians did not generate an indigence holy book, by the time they achieved the literacy in the early 19th century, and then most of them had converted into Islam. Nevertheless, the heritage of those far away days has been protected in mythology, giving us sight into the world of the prehistoric ancestors of the Circassians. In addition, the accounts of indigenous writers of the 19th century and foreign visitors entirely the ages provide snippets of pre-Islamic spiritual practices and ceremonies (Jaimoukha, 2001: pp. 137-138).

Some researcher such as *Amjad Jaimoukha* believes that there was some likeness between old Circassian priests and Celtic Druids[85]. Both castes glorified trees had sacred groves and practiced some form of human immolation and

---

84. In Circassian: Нартхымэ акъыбарыхэ *nartkhime akibarikhe* that are a series of tales originating from north Caucasus and form the basic mythology of the tribes and ethnics.
85. A druid was a member of the high-ranking professional class in ancient Celtic cultures.

sacrifice. In addition, the Circassian *Elders* and *Druids* were the arbitrators and judges in their respective societies (Jaimoukha, 2009: p. 06).

The *Animism*[86] is probably the oldest belief of the Circassians, and it was prevalent among all peoples of the North Caucasus. Its origin probably dates back to the Paleolithic Age, or the Old Stone Age, more than 10,000 years ago. The Circassians, similar the most North Caucasian peoples, used to praise the trees and considered them as totems, believing that they accommodated hidden divinity. Many ritual services were developed connected with specific plants such as trees and holy groves were visited by prayers in processions. Animals also were sacrificed at the bottom of trees and feasts held in the ceremony.

The route moved from *Animism* and the accompanying *Totemism*[87] into *Paganism*, the belief in the possession of some objects of supernatural powers nature, and a preliminary conception of deities and patrons. Perhaps paganism set up in the *Neolithic Age*, more than seven millennia ago. As a rule of thumb, every natural phenomenon had its own god. The collective of deities, gods, and patrons, who were part of the environment and supervised all its figures in a plural manner, formed a *Pantheon* with a leading god (Ibid: pp. 138-141). Therefore, like other Caucasian people, ancient beliefs had been influences on the Circassian identity, rather than adhering to official religions. Originally based on geography and environment, which has always been a place of transition, this religious identity has been formed.

About pre-Islamic beliefs, I should mention *Giorgio Interiano*'s text, which had this to say commenting on the religiousness of Circassians in the 16th century: "They call themselves Christians and have Greek clergymen among them, but they baptize their children after the age of 8. That said the clergymen just sprinkle them with holy water, in accordance with their custom, and utter a brief blessing" (Interiano, 1974: p. 47). The Christianity came to Western Circassia from Byzantium during the reign of Emperor Justinian[88] in the 6th century. Many clergyman and priests were sent to Circassia and Caucasus and then churches were built on some highland locations, from which the native

---

86. Animism is the religious belief that objects, places and creatures all possess a distinct spiritual essence. The basic tenet of animism was the belief that a soul resided in every object, animate or inanimate, functioning as the motive force and guardian. In animistic thought, nature was all alive. In a future state, the spirit would exist as part of an immaterial soul. The spirit, therefore, was thought to be universal. Ghosts, demons, and deities inhabited almost all objects, rendering them subject to worship.
87. Totemism, defined as the intimate relation supposed to exist between an individual or a group of individuals and a class of natural objects, i. e. the totem, is at the root of primitive religion and is intimately related with animism.
88. Justinian I in Latin: *Flavius Petrus Sabbatius Iustinianus Augustus* (482 - 565), known as Justinian the Great and also Saint Justinian the Great in the Eastern Orthodox Church, who was the Eastern Roman emperor from 527 to 565.

population was proselytized. The *Georgian Bagrationi dynasty*[89] subdued the Eastern Circassians and probably converted them to Greek Orthodox Christianity in the 13th century. Many Churches were built, which were destroyed at the end of Georgian rule in the 15th century. Additionally, some sources clarify that in the 11th and 12th centuries the Russian imperial princes of *Tmutarakan*[90] and the kings of Georgia executed the religious conversion in the course of Circassia. From the 13th to 15th centuries, *Catholicism* made some incursions in the Western parts of Circassia due to the influence of the *Genoese*, who created trading posts on the littoral of the Black Sea and even some churches were constructed in the region (Jaimoukha, 2009: pp. 5-8).

Islam

Islam is located in the center of Circassian religious identity nowadays. The Circassians are nominally Sunni Muslims of the Hanafi School, except for a small Orthodox Christian Kabardian community who are living in the city of *Mozdok*[91] in the North Ossetia. Islam almost began to make progress in Circassia around the 18th and 19th centuries. In the beginning, Islam had tiny influences on the folklore and writing traditions, but the only significant impact of the Muslim faith was the introduction of a new literary genre and sort, in the name of *Mevlid*[92], connected with the birth celebration of *Prophet Mohammad* (R. Smeets, 1980).

Generally, there were two types of *Muslimness* permeation of the Northern Caucasus. In the east, the first contact with Islam is accomplished in the 7th century when the Arabs conquered Dagestan. Progressively, Islam outspread to another part of North Caucasus. Thus by the 15th century, most lands of Northeast Caucasus had been converted to Islam by force or voluntarily. Therefore, Kabardians was the first among the Circassian people to be treated with the Islamic influences from the East. In 1570, *Giray*[93], the Khan of the Tatars, defeated a composed force of Beslanays and Kabardians, and forced some princes to become Muslim. Historically, the Ottomans, after conquering *Trebizond* in 1461, extended their domination over the entire coast and inland

---

89. In Georgian: ბაგრატიონი *bagrat'ioni* is a royal family that reigned in Georgia from the middle Ages until the early 19th century.
90. Tmutarakan or Tmutorakan was the name of a Mediaeval Kievan Rus' principality and trading town that controlled the Cimmerian Bosporus, the passage from the Black Sea to the Sea of Azov.
91. In Russian: Моздок *Mozdak* is a town and the administrative center of Mozdoksky District of the Republic of North Ossetia–Alania, Russia, located on the left shore of the Terek River.
92. In Arabic: المولد *mawlid*
93. Girays, were the Genghisid/Turkic dynasty that reigned in the Khanate of Crimea from its formation in 1427 until its downfall in 1783.

into Circassia. In these areas, the local aristocracy adopted Sunni Islam but the mass of the population was only lightly converted (Henze, 1995: p. 04).

The religious contest between Orthodox and Islam Sunni in Circassia caused an encounter between the two faiths. However, it was never serious religious quarrel, and it made only contacts with the Ottomans and the Russians in the 18th and 19th centuries by sending missionaries (Tarran, 1991: pp. 103-117). Nevertheless, by the middle of the 19th century, the most Circassians had become Muslims. We should not forget that due to the Caucasian war, which had to do with the activity of the so-called *Sheikh Mansour*[94]. Following overmuch armed clashes and the defeat of the Circassian originality, a new system of religious rules was established in Circassia, which now included four books: *The Bible*, *The Psalms of David*, *The evangelist's book*, and *The Quran* (Bell, 2007: p. 192).

After the exile, the destinies of the immigrants and those who remained took different routes. The recent group was disconnected from further Muslim influences and the ancient system of faiths importuned. Only a minority performed Islamic mores and rituals. Northwest Caucasians are not known for their religious fervor, nor do they display fundamentalist tendencies. Islam in the Circassian Republics has thus far not been radicalized such as Eastern Caucasus. Most religious instructors who were sent to the North Caucasus from the Middle East starting from the early 1990s realized that the Eastern North Caucasus a more fertile soil for their ritual teachings. In this regard, it is indispensable to emphasize the discrepancy between the religious faiths and practices of the Northeast and Northwest Caucasians. Islam formed as a fundamental part of the social and spiritual life in the east. There has developed a combination of Islam and the old beliefs culminating in Sufism and the *Tarikat*[95]. These sights have never met ground among the Circassians in the west who saw the new faith as a threat to their traditions and norms (Jaimoukha, 2001: p. 155).

The Circassian Diaspora tend to be more religious than those in the Caucasus are, although the survival and strength of ancient beliefs among the latter definitely deserve investigation. This reality has been generating some attrition and friction between the two sides. Most diaspora visitors scowled upon some of the old customs and traditions of Circassians that violated Islamic law *'Sharia'*. The terminating in tension is a consequence of the congested differences between these two groups. As Jaimoukha believes that the status will be under control for the near future owing to the small number of returnees to their

---

94. Al-Imam al-Mansur al-Mutawakil 'ala Allah known as Sheikh al-Mansur (1760–1794) was a Chechen Islamic religious and Military leader who led the resistance against Catherine the Great during the late 18th century.

95. In Arabic: طريقت *Tariqat*

homeland. However, if the number is ever to rise considerably, and afterward tension might expand into hatred, not to say as a conflict, which would defeat the whole purpose of the exercise (Jaimoukha, 2009: pp. 75-83). Nevertheless, a possible consideration for this contention, in addition to the applications of the community, might have been to attenuate the religious component which had supplied a connection to the Islam, and to accent the unique cultural-national component or perhaps an understanding and a recognition with the propensity to use the *United Language* as a tool to renew and to fasten ethnolinguistic identity.

Language & Literature

Language and literature are the means by which the cultural identity of a group people is comprehended and described. It is the storage of the spirit among a nation, an ethnic or a group of people and plays important role in the ethnolinguistic course.

The Circassian language as it is mentioned earlier is one of the three divisions of the Northwest Caucasian languages which usually calls *Adyghean*. Although genetically related with two others of *Abkhaz-Abaza* and extinct language of *Ubykh*, the three languages are reciprocally complex and unintelligible, the literal differences between them being quite fundamental. However, because of geographical gaps, the route language differentiated into three distinct existences: *proto-Abkhaz*, *proto-Circassian* and *proto-Ubykh* (Table. 07).

The Circassian literary language officially was promoted and formed after the October revolution of 1917. At the first in 1918, it developed based on Arabic script. The Latin script was adopted in 1927, and Cyrillic has been used since 1938 (Kuipers, 1960: pp. 07-10). The Circassian language itself is set up of Eastern and Western groups. The east of Circassia is combined of two main dialects, *Beslanay* and *Kabardian*. But, these dialects are too near that some linguists consider the latter a disparate sub-dialect of the former. In the west shows more marked dialect-divisions than Kabardian, which is overall relatively homogeneous. These are differences and names all because of a reflection to the tribal and social structures between Eastern and Western Circassians (Map. 07).

Each branch of Circassian is demonstrated by one literary and official language: Kabardian in *Kabardin-Balkar* and the *Karachay-Cherkess Republics*, and *Adyghean* in the *Adyghea Republic*. Literary Kabardian is based on the dialect of *Greater Kabardia*[96]. Literary *Adyghea* is an advanced form of

---

96. Or Kabarda which refers to Easter Circassia as a historical land.

Temirgoi, with a substantive input of words and forms from *Bzhedugh* and *Shapsug*. In fact, according to Jaimoukha's opinion, the modern West Circassian is based on the dialects of remained tribes after the exile which has escaped the worst (Jaimoukha, 2001: pp. 245-249).

In the case of literature, according to the German scholar, *F. Bodenstedt*, who visited the North Caucasus at the beginning of the 19th century, mentioned that for the Circassian, the poetry is a reservoir of national wisdom, a guide to decent action, and the definitive arbiter (Jaimoukha, 2001). On the other hand, *Paul B. Henze* wrote, "Circassians had a rich tradition of oral poetry. Oratory was a highly developed art. Leaders gained as much renowned for their speechmaking ability as for their skill in battle" (Henze, 1992: p. 71). Additionally, *W. E. Curtis*, who traveled to the North Caucasus in the 20th century, asserted that Circassia did not have literature, but "their poets have written many charming lines and there are two or three local histories of merit" (Curtis, 1911: p. 255). His report was protecting, to say the least, and ejected writing traditions that drawback for hundreds of years.

In fact, Circassian literature was written well before the Russian invasion of Northwest Caucasus and certainly had attained a high level of development long before the Russians made their presence felt in the 16th century. It had been preserved in national memory thanks to the roving musicians. Linguistically, some tales go back almost 1,500 years, to the time of early Christianity in the Northwest Caucasus. Some efforts to collect these tales first was in 1860 by *V. Kusikov* who published '*On the Poetry of the Circassians*' in Stavropol. Later in 1924, a collection of *Adyghean* literary material was published in Moscow. Additionally, work on the history of Kabardian literature had already been published by *Chamozokov*[97] by 1929. Generally, oral tradition consists of thousands of tales and stories that take up almost every theme in the life of ancient Circassians. When literature was formalized in the Soviet Union era, writers had a very rich tradition to fall back upon, and many mature works were produced early on. In fact, they can be considered as a continuance of the old structure. In spite of the limitations imposed by ideology and the narrow scope of permissible themes, classic works were penned that have kept their value to this day (Jaimoukha, 1998, p. 02).

---

97. See more details: *Chamozokov, 'Istoriya kabardinskoi pismennosti [History of Kabardian Writers]', in Zapiski SeveroKavkazskogo Kraevogo gorskogo nauchno-issledovatelskogo instituta, Rostov-on-Don, vol. 2, 1929.*

Ethno-Political Issues

If we want to talk about ethnopolitical issues as the most part of Human Geography in Circassia or better to say in the Northwest Caucasus, at first we should refer to the end of Soviet Union or even further till the announcement of the 'Declaration on the State Sovereignty of the Russian Federation'[98] which was an intensive search for ways to reform the nation-state mechanism of the Russian Federation hegemony. Additionally, I should draw the attention that between 1990 and 1996, the formation of politicized national movements with the ideas about reforming the national-state system in the Northwest Caucasus was completed. Projects for the division, or federalization, of the republics of *Kabardin-Balkar* and *Karachay-Cherkess* in accordance with ethnic principles were put forward. It means authorities had already decided not to have two homogeneous ethnic republics, for example, *Kabardin-Cherkess* and *Karachay-Balkar*.

Roman Szporluk believes that one of the characteristic aspects of the Soviet theory and practice in the field of the nationality-citizenship question was that "it virtually created nations and nationalities following criteria and purposes that were its own, and in conformity with these it charted out 'national' or 'republic' borders. The Soviets thus created a host of ethnic problems that they proved to be incapable of dealing with in the final years of the USSR and left as their legacy to their successors. One of the fundamental aspects of the entire Soviet experience with ethnicity was to connect nationality and the right of nationalities to the territory. The Soviets did not invent the concept of ethnic homeland, but they did much to make it even more central to the idea of nationality than it had been earlier... All those ethnic homelands enjoyed under the Soviets the status of political entities, and even the smallest, and thus ranking lowest in the hierarchy of autonomous regions and republics, formally enjoyed at least rudiments of 'statehood" (Szporluk, 1994: p. 05).

Therefore, diversity in religion, ethnicity, historical experience, and political allegiances and aspirations complicate efforts to alleviate local tensions and integrate it more with the rest of the country. Understanding this pluralism is essential for designing and implementing policies and laws that advance conflict resolution rather than make differences more irreconcilable (International Crisis Group, 2012).

---

98. The Declaration of State Sovereignty of the Russian SFSR (Russian: Декларация о государственном суверенитете РСФСР, tr. Deklaratsiya o gosudarstvennom suverenitete RSFSR) was a political act of the Russian SFSR (Russian Soviet Federative Socialist Republic), then part of the Soviet Union, which marked the beginning of constitutional reform in Russia. (12 June 1990)

In *Kabardin-Balkar*, the *Balkar national movement* demanded the formation of a Federal Republic of *Kabardia* and *Balkaria* in which the minority *Balkars* would enjoy both full equality and virtually complete autonomy. Later, the Kabardian and the *Balkarian movements* went even further and agreed to the dissolution of the *Kabardin-Balkar Republic,* an agreement that was supported by the Supreme Soviet of the *Kabardin-Balkar Republic*. All of this created an enormously unstable ethnolinguistic situation (Azrael and others, 1998: pp. 45-48) (Table. 08).

Popov an ethnic researcher in Russia thinks those issues come from identity-based interaction which implies ambiguous, contradictory and diametrically opposite effects on the same political, cultural and historical contexts. On the one hand, the identity-based interactions contribute to the development of civic consciousness, increasing the social importance of an individual and the level of political rights and freedoms. The necessity of promoting the ethnopolitical integration in the Northwest Caucasus is due to instrumental causes: from the ethic viewpoint which the main one is ethnolinguistic, the creation of an integrated 'society for everyone' is natural societal purpose; the constructional reasons of supporting the integration are connected with social, economic, ethnic contradistinctions that diminish the mobility, which in its turn leads to social atomization and produces a negative effect on the modernization process and prevention of ethnic conflicts in their most destructive form of identity-based conflicts (Popov, 2017: pp. 76-77).

Another important point is this case is religion, basically Islam. It is quite possible that demographical growth will continue especially in Muslims case what will lead to greater press on limited economical sources and more intensive interethnic competition in Circassia. This matter is important to attend to growing Islam influence among young Circassian generations. The religion can become both an ethnic identity base and an efficient move of Circassian mobilization against external policy from Moscow.

The latest ethnopolitical issues, in the case of Sochi Olympic, several Circassian diaspora activists were disenchanted with the meager results of the campaigns against the sports events hosted in Sochi. The failure to fully accomplish the ethnopolitical agenda post-Sochi Winter Olympic and Paralympic Games and post-May 21 do not have to mean the end game for Circassian activists across the diaspora and/or living in the homeland. Generally, it was characterized as disrespect of Circassian ancestors. Emotional perception of history carried a unifying function; it contributed to ethnic mobilization and politicization (Petersson & Vamling, 2013: pp. 95-123), though the emotional background was successfully combined with pragmatism. The Sochi Olympics also were supposed to bring to Circassians, much more globally and universal (Muller, 2013: pp. 5-14). Therefore, it can be concluded that, especially since the collapse of the Soviet Union, the ethnic-political issues in the region has been pursued in a sensitive manner. Even though the partition of cultural and linguistic groups into definite and reciprocally limited ethnic categories is an optional process, this can be gained by examining undeniable specification systematically in all cases. In this case, the Circassian Diaspora acted the opportunities provided by the upcoming an international event as the very chance for the manifestation of their right for the territory of Circassia to the international community (Tsibenko, 2015: p. 83). In addition, the polar attitude of ethnopolitical issues manifested itself toward the Circassian Question and requiring immediate solution by means of the research activity, in Russia, on the contrary, its very existence was placed in question. In general speaking, I think the ethnolinguistic phenomena are base and route of all ethnopolitical issues in the whole region of Caucasus.

2 Chapter - Historical Background

Introduction

The Circassians have had the complicated background and few historical written sources make difficult explore in their history for historians. Since the beginning of their history, they lived on their lands in a tribal or clan structure and organized their societies according to their traditions and customs as mentioned in the previous chapter. In this chapter, I will survey their historical background until Circassians exile by the Imperial Russian Army, and when they became a part of the Ottoman population. Although their highland homeland is well-known for its uneven, isolating topography, the Circassians have long been well consolidated with the international arena. Circassia faces a large expansion of the Black Sea, a region that has attracted regional merchants and neighboring settlers specifically from the Greek world and beyond. In the later Middle Ages and into early modern times, *Genoese* traders frequented the coastal of Circassian territories. Politically, the region is usually demonstrated as a backwater, as the Circassians never created a powerful state of their own (Lewis, 2012).

Throughout the development stages of the Circassian Question and the transformation of its perception clearly, show the certain constants in the international position on the Russian and the Ottoman presence in the Caucasus. In the 18th and 19th centuries, the Circassian question was repeatedly actualized in connection with geopolitical turbulence, provoking crises in international relations. Turning into a tool for the political push in the conflict for sovereignty, the Circassian Question punctually withdrew into the shades at the consolidation and stabilization of the geopolitical region (Gody, 2015: pp. 45-6). The most prominent feature of this historical period in this chapter is the series of wars between Russian and Circassian and the trans-regional developments surrounding the Circassia and the Caucasus.

Additionally, I try to identify Circassian historical background according to the primary and secondary sources. Using the term Circassian as a historical category of identification, the aim of this chapter is to explore the history of Circassians in general and explore the factors that contribute to the creation of Circassian identity in the later phase, specifically the relations between the Circassian identity and Circassian Question. Therefore, I focused on three parts, first of all, the historical background of Circassians before the 18th century, second I will deepen for analyzing the situation of Circassia and the Northwest

Caucasus in the 18th and 19th centuries which I think it was the most important stage in the Circassian history, and then finally I will highlight the policies of regional and trans-regional actors and players in the term of *Circassian Question* formation.

Rise up in the History

It is possible that most probably the ancestors of the Circassians have had contacts with the peoples who have passed across the steppes from the North and across the mountain from the South such as Indo-Europeans[99] including *Cimmerians*[100], *Scythians*[101], *Sarmatians*[102], *Alans*[103], *Iranians*[104], *Greeks*[105] and *Goths*[106]; and *Altaic*[107] people including *Huns*[108], *Khazars*[109], *Mongols*[110]; and lastly *Slavs*[111] such as *Cossacks*[112], *Ukrainians*[113], and *Russians*[114]. The communications and the interactions on these millennia were more linked to the exchange of cultural and linguistic issues, which can be obvious in the indigenous culture of North Caucasian people.

---

99. The *Proto-Indo-Europeans* were the prehistoric people of Eurasia who spoke Proto-Indo-European (PIE), the ancestor of the Indo-European languages according to linguistic reconstruction.
100. The *Kimmerians* were an ancient people, who appeared about 1000 BC and are mentioned later in 8th century BC in Assyrian records.
101. Or the *Scyths* were a group of Iranian people, known as the Eurasian nomads, who inhabited the western and central Eurasian steppes from about the 9th century BC until about the 1st century BC. Scythia was the Greek term for the grasslands north and east of the Black Sea. The *Scythian* languages belonged to the Eastern branch of the Iranian languages.
102. The *Sarmatians* were a large Iranian confederation that existed in classical antiquity, flourishing from about the 5th century BC to the 4th century AD.
103. Or the *Alani* were an Iranian nomadic pastoral people of antiquity and most possibly related to the *Massagetae*. The name Alan is an Iranian dialectical form of Aryan, a common self-designation of the Indo-Iranians.
104. An *Indo-European* ethno-linguistic group compromising the speakers of the Iranian languages including Iran and other nations in Central Asia, and the Middle East.
105. Or the *Hellenes* are an ethnic group native to Greece, Cyprus, southern Albania, Italy, Turkey, or Egypt, to a lesser extent, other countries surrounding the Mediterranean Sea.
106. The *Goths* were an East Germanic people, two of whose branches, the Visigoths and the Ostrogoths, played an important role in the fall of the Western Roman Empire and the emergence of Medieval Europe.
107. The *Altaic* is a proposed language family of central Eurasia and Siberia, now widely seen as discredited. The Turkic, Mongolic and *Tungusic* groups are invariably included in the family; some authors added Korean and *Japonic* languages.
108. The *Huns* were a nomadic people who lived in Eastern Europe, the Caucasus, and Central Asia between the 4th century AD and the 6th century AD.
109. The *Khazars* were a semi-nomadic Turkic people, who created what for its duration was the most powerful polity to emerge from the break-up of the *Western Turkic Kaganate*.
110. The *Mongols* are an East-Central Asian ethnic group native to Mongolia and China's Inner Mongolia Autonomous Region.
111. The *Slavs* are the largest Indo-European ethno-linguistic group who speak the various Slavic languages of the larger Balto-Slavic linguistic group.
112. The *Cossacks* were a group of predominantly East Slavic-speaking people who became known as members of democratic, self-governing, semi-military communities, predominantly located in Southern Russia and in South-Eastern Ukraine.
113. The *Ukrainians* are an East Slavic ethnic group native to Ukraine.
114. The *Russians* are an East Slavic ethnic group native to Eastern Europe.

In my opinion, for the beginning, I should draw the Circassia in the site of the Bronze Age which mostly is characterized by *Maykop culture*[115] (3700 BC – 2200 BC) and later *Koban culture*[116] (1400 BC - 400 BC). Actually, the *Maykop culture* influences were mostly on the peoples who lived across the Koban plain where was a major Bronze Age archaeological culture in the western Caucasus region of southern Russia (Ivanova, 2007: pp. 7-39) (Map. 08). From the late second to early first millennium BC, the Koban tribes achieved a high level of cultural developments and they maintained commercial links with *Transcaucasia* (Jaimoukha, 2001: pp. 38-39), then we see the growth of *Koban Culture* (Figure. 06) at the late Bronze Age and Iron Age culture of the northern and central Caucasus. It is preceded by the *Colchian* culture of the western Caucasus and the Kharachoi culture[117] further east (Jaimoukha, 2004: pp. 23-28). Both of these cultures depended on the continuous flow of metal objects, especially weapons and their inhumation practices were characteristically Indo-European, typically in a pit, sometimes stone-lined, topped with a kurgan[118] (Vasmer, 1953-1958: p. 24). The Circassia in Bronze and Iron Ages was extremely rich in gold and silver artifacts; unusual for the time (Kohl, 2014; Gobejishvili, 2014) (Figure. 07).

The Iron Ages in the Northwest Caucasus and in the Circassia began about 8th century BC. Some archeologists' founding has been attributed to the *Proto-Circassian* or *Proto-Maeotian* Culture. Their civilization lasted for some 1,200 years and their state was contemporaneous with Greek colonies, which were established in the 7th and 6th centuries BC (Jaimoukha, 2001: pp. 42-43).

From this centuries, common influences between the Caucasian and Iranian origins persisted, which fact can be corroborated by the wealth of artifacts of the *Maeotian*[119]-*Scythian* period that goes back to late seventh to fourth centuries BC, and to the *Maeotian-Sarmatian* period, from the last few centuries BC to the first few centuries AD. Therefore, I can conclude that the first bearers of the population were aboriginals in the Caucasus, who crossed the Don at the time of great *Sarmatian Migration*, together with the *Ants, Zikhis (Kissis), Chorvats, Vals*, and other small tribes (Map. 09) (Ibid: p. 36).

---

115. In Russian: Майкопская культура (3700 BC—3000 BC), was a major Bronze Age archaeological culture in the Western Caucasus region of Southern Russia.
116. Or Kuban in Russian: Кобанская культура (1100 to 400 BC), was a late Bronze Age and Iron Age culture of the northern and central Caucasus.
117. The term Kharachoi culture denotes the Early Bronze Age of Chechnya. Clay jugs and stone grain containers indicate a high level of development of trade and culture.
118. In English, the archaeological term kurgan is a loanword from East Slavic languages, equivalent to the archaic English term barrow, also known by the Latin loanword tumulus and terms such as burial mound. These are structures created by heaping earth and stones over a burial chamber, which is often made of wood.
119. The *Maeotians* were an ancient people dwelling along the Sea of Azov, which was known in antiquity as the "Maeotian marshes" or "Lake Maeotis". For more information, you can see: Boardman, John; Edwards, I. E. S. (1991). The Cambridge Ancient History. Volume 3. Part 2. Cambridge University Press.

By the fifth century BC, the Sindis[120], people kindred to the *Maeots*, had set up the magnificent *Sindica* civilization, which spread over the lower reaches of the Kuban, the Black Sea coastal strip between Anapa and Taman Peninsula, inclusive (Ibid, p. 43).

Generally, the early history of the Circassian peoples is obscure, but since 4th century BC, they have been witnessing a widespread wave of invaders and immigrants to the Northwest Caucasus. Historically, first time was by the *Sarmatians*[121] who started migrating westward, coming to dominate the closely related *Scythians* to the Northwest Caucasus. Archeologically, the Greeks also were known and were the first state to have established colonies and carried out extensive trade on the Circassian coast of the Black Sea, and their influence is still clear. Because of Greek and Byzantine influence, later Christianity spread throughout the Northwest Caucasus between the 3-5th centuries (Minahan, 2000: p. 354).

The *Hun* invasion of the Northwest Caucasus in 374 AD caused the hinterland *Maeotians* to remove to the safety of the mountains. Attila attached twice to Circassian lands, the first time they routed and had to flee to the safety of *Elbrus* (Map. 10). The *Hun Hordes*, inebriated by their might, swarmed up the heights but were overwhelmed by the agile defenders who were familiar with every nook and cranny. The Hun army was crushed and they expelled. The Byzantine Empire secured a foothold in the western Caucasus in the 4th century. Fortresses were erected on the Black Sea coast and the *Taman Peninsula* (Jaimoukha, 2001: pp. 45-46).

This process was taken by the Bulgars[122] almost after the *Roman Era*. The *Bulgar state*, with its capital at *Phanagoria*[123], reached the apex of its geopolitical sway from 632 to 668 AD, as *Old Great Bulgaria*[124] (Leif Inge Ree, 2013: p. 112). Under push from the Khazars[125] side, *Great Bulgaria* rejected quickly and collapsed, to be made out by the *Khazar Khaganate*[126] in 668. The

---

120. The *Sindi* were an ancient people in the Taman Peninsula and the adjacent coast of the Pontus Euxinus (Black Sea), in the district called Sindica, which spread between the modern towns of Temryuk and Novorossiysk.
121. The *Sarmatians* were a large Iranian confederation that existed in classical antiquity, flourishing from about the 5th century BC to the 4th century AD.
122. The *Bulgars* were Turkic semi-nomadic warrior tribes that flourished in the Pontic-Caspian steppe and the Volga region and north Caucasus during the 4th till 7th century.
123. *Phanagoria* in ancient Greek: Φαναγόρεια *Phanagóreia*, was the largest ancient Greek city on the Taman peninsula, spread over two plateaus along the eastern shore of the Cimmerian Bosporus.
124. Old Great Bulgaria or Great Bulgaria in Byzantine Greek: Παλαιά Μεγάλη Βουλγαρία, *Palaiá Megálē Voulgaría*, also often known by the Latin names Magna Bulgaria and Patria Onoguria land, was a 7th Century state formed by the Bulgars and Onogurs on the western Pontic Steppe (modern southern Ukraine and south-west Russia).
125. The Khazars were a semi-nomadic Turkic people, who created what for its duration was the most powerful polity to emerge from the break-up of the Western Turkic Kaganate.
126. Or *Qağanate*

Circassia, following the dissolution of the *Khazar Khaganate*, were integrated by the *Kingdom of Alania*[127] at the 8th and 9th centuries (Map. 11) (Zuckerman, 2007: p. 417).

This land remained fairly autonomous until the 12th and 13th centuries, when Georgian princes, specifically the Reign of *Queen Tamar*[128] (Figure. 08), succeeded in reducing it to the condition of a province (Map. 12). Therefore, the *Georgian Kingdom* had an influence on the Circassia, adopting Christianity. Even the architecture of Circassian Church at that time is very similar to Georgians. This was the peak of Georgian authority, which expanded over most of the Caucasus. Circassia rebelled against Georgian rule towards the end of the 14th century, but around 1390, during the rule of *King Bagrat VI*[129], the Georgians mounted a punitive campaign against the insurrectionists and took many hostages (Jaimoukha, 2001: p. 48).

During the 13th and 14th centuries, the Northwest Caucasus was overrun by *Mongol Hordes*, who launched two long massive invasions toward Circassia. In 1237, the assault on the North Caucasus began as the first Mongol Invasion (Anchalabze, 2001: p. 24). There is an important text by *William Rubruck*[130], the envoy of the French Kingdom to *Sartaq Khan*[131], traveled to the North Caucasus in 1253 about this invasion. He wrote that the Circassians had never 'bowed to Mongol rule', despite the fact that whole fifth of the Mongol armies was at that time dedicated to the task of squashing the whole of North Caucasian resistance (Jaimoukha, 2004: pp. 34-35). The second Mongol invasion was just as brutal as the first and happened by *Timurlane*[132] who first sent his Turkic tribe fighters and warriors to invade in 1390, and profoundly stepped up the invasion in 1395-1396 (Map. 13) (Anchalabze, 2001: p. 25). After these two invasions, the Northwest Caucasus soon passed under the rule of the Crimean Tatars and later under the rule of the Ottoman Empire. Under the influence of these two Muslim states, Circassian society started to adopt Islam.

Nevertheless, the Circassians not only in the Caucasus, but even farther away in the Middle East and the North Africa had influenced and connected as

---

127. Alania was a medieval kingdom of the Iranian Alans that flourished in the Northern Caucasus, roughly in the location of latter-day Circassia and modern North Ossetia–Alania, from the 8th or 9th century until its destruction by the Mongol invasion in 1238-39.
128. Tamar the Great (c. 1160 – 18 January 1213) reigned as the Queen of Georgia from 1184 to 1213, presiding over the apex of the Georgian Golden Age. For more information, you can see: Dondua, Varlam; Berdzenishvili, Niko (1985). Жизнь царицы цариц Тамар (The Life of the Queen of Queens Tamar). Tbilisi: Metsniereba.
129. Bagrat VI (c. 1439 – 1478), a representative of the *Imeretian branch of the Bagrationi royal house*, was a king of Imereti from 1463, and a king of Georgia from 1465 until his death.
130. William of Rubruck (c. 1220 – c. 1293) was a Flemish Franciscan missionary and explorer.
131. Sartaq Khan (died 1256) was the son of *Batu Khan* and Regent Dowager Khatun Boraqcin of Alchi Tatar. He succeeded Batu as khan of the Golden Horde.
132. Timur in Persian: تيمورTemūr (1336 – 1405), historically known as *Amir Timur* and was a Turco-Mongol conqueror. As the founder of the Timurid Empire in Persia and Central Asia, he became the first ruler in the Timurid dynasty.

between 1382 and 1517 and formed the *Burji dynasty*[133] under *Mamluk Sultanate*[134] that ruled over Egypt which it traces even older back to 1297 when Lajin[135] became Sultan of *Mamluk Sultanate* (McGregor, 2006: p. 15). Although the make-up of the *Burji Mamluk* dynasty was mostly Circassians, there were also Abkhaz, Abaza, and Georgians whom the Arab Sultans recruited to serve their kingdoms as a military force (Isichei, 1997: p.192) (Map. 14). They were deeply rooted in Egyptian society and the history of the region as well as for centuries; they have been part of the ruling elite in Egypt, having served in the high military, political and social positions. There is some evidence of linking between these *Mamelukes* and the *Kabardians'* expansion in the 14th century eastward of the Caucasus. In spite of noncentralized state, the *Kabardians* organized a homogeneous political unit like a state, whilst the other Circassians remained around tribal and clan schemas.

The 16th & 17th centuries can be named as the beginning of the struggle ages over the Caucasus among the regional powers, including the *Persians*, the *Russians*, and the *Ottomans* and it is an era of first Circassian immigration to the Middle East. The era when the Circassians mostly worked as military in the regional armies and Circassia was in the middle of their battles. For example, only the *Safavid*[136] (1501–1736) dynasty saw the importing and deporting of large numbers of Circassians to Persia, where many enjoyed prestige in the harems and in the *élite armies*[137], while many others settled and deployed as craftsmen, laborers, farmers, and regular soldiers.

In the late 1550s, the ruler of one of the Kabardian noble families, Kemirgoquo[138], struck a politico-military alliance with *Tsar Ivan IV*[139], for mutual assistance against expansionist attacks by the Persian and Ottoman Empires and the Tatars. It seems that those Circassians involved in this alliance were Christians (Shenfield, 1999: p.150). Almost in the 16th century, Russia started pushing southwards the Caucasians in a process of continuous violations. In 1570, the Khan of the Tatars, threatened by the Russian encroachment,

---

133. The *Burji* dynasty (Arabic: المماليك البرجية) was a Circassian Mamluk dynasty which ruled Egypt
134. The Mamluk Sultanate (1250–1517) in Arabic: سلطنة المماليك *Saltanat al-Mamālīk*, was a medieval realm spanning Egypt, the Levant, and Hejaz.
135. Lachin in Arabic: لاجين *Lajin*, full royal name al-Malik al-Mansour Hossam ad-Din Lachin al-Mansuri who was a Mamluk sultan of Egypt from 1296 to 1299.
136. The *Safavid dynasty* in Persian: دودمان صفوی *Dudmān e Safavi*, was one of the most significant ruling dynasties of Iran, often considered the founding of modern Iranian history. For more information, you can see: Streusand, Douglas E. (2011). Islamic Gunpowder Empires: Ottomans, Safavids, and Mughals. Boulder, Col: Westview Press.
137. So-called *Ghulams*
138. Under *Temriuk* Prince
139. Ivan IV Vasilyevich in Russian: Иван Васильевич, commonly known as *Ivan the Terrible* or Ivan the Fearsome, was the Grand Prince of Moscow from 1533 to 1547, then Tsar of All the Russia until his death in 1584.

gathered a great force and marched on the lands of five mountains[140]. The Circassians were crushed and the victorious Khan forced some of them to embraced Islam and resettle on the bank of the *Kuban river*. The Russian bid to subdue the North Caucasus was checked in 1605 when a combined force of the *Shamkhal*[141] of Dagestan and the Ottomans dealt a severe blow to Tsarist ambitions. However, the Cossacks kept their presence in the area, but they were not yet under direct Russian influence (Jaimoukha, 2001: p. 52). Thereafter, raids and counter-raids became the order of the day. In 1712, the Cossacks submitted to Tsar Peter the Great[142] and were incorporated into Russian war machine in the southern borders. They become a potent force in the Russian relentless drive to warm waters, playing a major part in the Caucasian War.

Circassia in 18th-19th Centuries

When Russian Empire ambitions brought their troops to the Caucasus in the late 17th and early 18th centuries, Circassia found a special situation among the Russo-Ottoman Wars[143] and the Russo-Persian Wars[144], actually it was located at the front of the battles. Therefore, the situation of Circassia in the 18th century was mostly characterized by the start of the Russo-Circassian War in 1763 and resistance movements for their identity. This century finally ends by the conquest of *Anapa*[145] and capture of *Sheikh Mansur*[146] in 1791.

In the 18th century, *Kabarda* extended across the central third of the north Caucasus piedmont from east of Circassia proper to the Chechen. The fort of *Mozdok* on the western side of *Terek* river was built in Kabardian territory and a line of fortress was check out the *Terek* to *Kizlyar*[147].

Generally, from the time of *Peter I*, the interest in the Caucasus grew. In his demand for outlets to the southern seas, *Peter I* had his eyes on the warm seas for sailing and shipping in all seasons. Progress in this direction met with the resistance of Ottoman and the Crimea. The expedition against Azov and its

---

140. Which calls now *Pyatigorsk* in Russian: Пятигорск is a city in Stavropol Krai.
141. *Shamkhal* is the title for the rulers of *Kumukh* in Dagestan during the 8th-17th centuries.
142. Peter the Great in Russian: Пётр Великий, ruled the Tsardom of Russia and later the Russian Empire from 7 May 1682 until his death in 1725. For more information, you can see: Anisimov, Evgenii V. (2015) The Reforms of Peter the Great: Progress through Violence in Russia (Routledge).
143. Or Ottoman–Russian wars were a series of wars between the Russian Empire and the Ottoman Empire between the 16th and 20th centuries. In this case, I mean the wars of 1768–1774 and 1787–1792.
144. Specifically on 1722–23 and 1796; for more detail you can see: Andreeva, Elena (2007). Russia and Iran in the Great Game: Travelogues and Orientalism. Routledge: p.38.
145. Anapa in Russian: *Анána*, is a town in Krasnodar Krai, Russia, located on the northern coast of the Black Sea near the Sea of Azov.
146. Sheikh al-Mansur (1760–1794) was a Chechen Islamic religious and military leader who led the Circassian and Caucasian resistance against Catherine the Great during the late 18th century.
147. In Russian: *Кизля́р*, is a town in the Republic of Dagestan, Russia, located on the border with the Chechen Republic in the delta of the Terek River.

capture in 1696 and the trade between Russia and Persia aggravated an age-old enmity. Ottoman Empire, through the Crimea, tried to consolidate its position there, particularly in Circassia. Thus, the Crimean Khans, *Qaplan I* Giray in 1707 and Saadet IV Giray in 1724 undertook devastating raids on Kabarda. The Crimean Khans, in their turn, pointed to the articles in the 1713 peace treaty, according to which the Circassia, including the Kabardians, were recognized as dependent on the Crimean Khan. Occasionally, the *Crimean Khans* attacked *Kabarda*, in order to consolidate the Muslim faith there by force, as was the case in 1717, when the *Crimean hordes* attended outside *Maykop*. On other episode, the wars between the *Porte* and *Persia* served as a excuse (Hammer-Purgstall, 1856: pp. 201-206). When the Porte declared war on Persia, the Sultan ordered *Qaplan I* Giray to advance on the Northern Caucasus and further on Persia (1733), which resulted in a war between Russia and the Crimea. This constant interference in Circassia affairs by *Turks* and *Crimeans* on the one hand and Russians on the other was also facilitated by internal strife in *Kabarda*. It is natural that the *Kabardian* issue should have been the object of negotiation and have found a place in the *Belgrade* peace treaty of September 18, 1739 (Namitok, 1956: p. 17).

In 1771, the Russians defeated the *Kabardians* on the *Malka River* and subjugated some of *Lesser Kabarda*. In 1777-78, the path was expanded from Mozdok northwest to the *Azov Sea*. In 1779, the *Kabardians* were beaten, failure of 50 princes and 350 nobles and a border was appointed along the *Malka* and *Terek* rivers. It might look that the Circassians should have organized a united state to oppose the Russians, but the reality of region remains that the unorganized Circassians overspread longer than the organized *Murids*. Then the territory of Circassians was gradually pushed toward the southern zones between 1763 and 1793. The Russians constructed a line of fortresses that were used as springboards for further outreach. By the end of the century, most of *Kabarda* was under imperial Russian control. Some Kabardians, later dubbed as *Muhajir*[148], immigrant or fugitive Circassians, who refused to accept Russian hegemony, moved west to what is now known as the *Karachay-Cherkess Republic* and the *Adyghea Republic*.

at the first quarter of the 19th century, the Russians built no viable gains in Circassia. In 1829, Ottoman gave Russia a free hand in the Caucasus in the treaty of Adrianople, in spite of the reality that the Ottomans had no assertion whatsoever Circassia. afterward, Russia embarked on a harsh war of abrasion,

---

148. *Muhajir* or *Mohajir* (Arabic: مهاجر muhājir; pl. مهاجرون muhājirūn) is an Arabic word meaning emigrant. In English, this term and its derivatives have been applied to a number of groups and individuals:
Muhacir (Turkish variant), Caucasian Muslims who immigrated to Anatolia, from the late 18th century until the end of the 20th century.

which met with furious resistance for 35 years. The odds were greatly accumulated against the Circassians, whose limited soldiers and manpower were no matches to the ongoing stream of cannon fodder unleashed at them. One is persuaded to say that the Circassians, to their mortal harm, had never really grasped the full bound of the cruelty of the Russian war machine.

The Circassians performed a notably savage and long-lasting resistance to Russian sovereignty. Disappointed by the occasional rekindling of resistance in apparently conciliated the Circassian villages, Russia in 1860 started a campaign to forcibly resettle Circassians eastbound of the Kuban River. By 1864, the removal had mostly been done, but nearly the entire Circassian population instead of immigrating to the Ottoman Empire, with many thousands dying of starvation and disease on the way. A report of this Circassian resistance has been written by *Henze* (1990), though many details remain to be documented.

Russo–Ottoman War

The Russo–Ottoman War[149] was a series of wars between the Russian Empire and the Ottoman Empire that happened from the 16th until 20th centuries in different parts of Eastern Europe and the Caucasus. It was one of the interminable series of armed conflicts in European history (Timothy, 2014). Since these wars have had a major impact on the *Circassian History* especially on the Russo-Circassian Wars, I am referring to this issue in this chapter. The most effective wars which had an impact on Circassian History, from my point of view were included of the Russo-Ottoman War from 1735 to 1739 with coagulation of Belgrade Treaty, Russo-Ottoman War from 1768 to 1774 with coagulation of Küçük Kaynarca Treaty, Russo-Ottoman War from 1787 to 1792 with coagulation of Jassy Treaty, Russo-Ottoman War from 1806 to 1812 with coagulation of Bucharest Treaty, Russo-Ottoman War from 1828 to 1829 with coagulation of Adrianople Treaty and finally Crimean War from 1853 to 1856 with coagulation of Paris Treaty. The process of wars caused the Russian Empire to reach the Ottoman borders in the Caucasus, where was located between three regional powers such as Persians, Ottomans, and Russians. Most probably could be concluded that the greatest impact was on Circassia, such that almost at the end of the Crimean War with coagulation of Paris Treaty in 1856, the Caucasian Wars and the Russo-Circassian Wars ended with catastrophic

---

149. Alternatively, the Russian - Turkish wars in Russian: Рýсско - Турéцкие вóйны and in Turkish: Osmanlı-Rus Savaşları.

results, and then the entire of North Caucasus was annexed to Russian Empire[150].

Belgrade Treaty (1739)

At the end of the Russo-Ottoman War (1735–1739) (Map. 15), the *Belgrade Treaty* known as the *Belgrade* peace treaty signed in Belgrade, *Habsburg Kingdom of Serbia*[151], by the Ottoman Empire on one side and the *Habsburg Monarchy*[152] on the other, which ended the *Austro-Turkish War* (1737–39) or *Austro-Russian-Turkish War* (1735–39) (Stone, 2006: p. 64). It should be noted that this war also represented Russia's continuing struggle for access to the Black Sea in the 18th century. During this war, there was another point, which happened in 1737, and Austria joined the war on Russia's side, therefore it is known in historiography as the Austro-Turkish War. This series of War begun because of the raids of the Crimean Tatars toward *Cossack Hetmanate*[153] at the end of 1735 and the Crimean khan's military campaign in the Caucasus. It made the Russian Dnieper Army react under the command of Field Marshal Burkhard Christoph von Münnich[154] and their attack to the Crimean fortifications at Perekop[155] and occupied Bakhchysarai[156] (Tucker, 2010: p. 732). In the resulting Belgrade treaty in 1739, for the first time the independence of Eastern Circassia where I mean *Kabarda* was formally guaranteed in the treaty by both sides (Hupchick, 2002: p.213). Article six of the Treaty stated: "As for the two Kabardas, Greater and Lesser, and the nations that inhabit therein, the two parties agree that the two Kabardias shall remain free, and will submit to neither of the two empires, but will be considered as a boundary between the two; and on the part of the Sublime Porte, neither the Turks nor the Tatars shall interfere in the internal affairs of these two countries, and, according to old custom, the

---

150. For more details: Aksan, Virginia (2007). Ottoman Wars, 1700–1860: An Empire Besieged. Pearson Education Ltd.
151. The Kingdom of Serbia was a province of the Habsburg monarchy from 1718 to 1739. It was formed from the territories to the south of the rivers Sava and Danube, corresponding to the Sanjak of Smederevo, conquered by the Habsburgs from the Ottoman Empire in 1717. It was abolished and returned to the Ottoman Empire in 1739.
152. The Habsburg Monarchy or Empire is an unofficial appellation among historians for the countries and provinces that were ruled by the junior Austrian branch of the House of Habsburg between 1521 and 1780 and then by the successor branch of Habsburg-Lorraine until 1918.
153. In Ukrainian: Гетьманщина, Het'manshchyna, known as the Ruthenian State or Zaporizhian Host, was a Ukrainian Cossack state in Central Ukraine between 1649 and 1764.
154. In Russian Христофо́р Анто́нович Ми́них (1683 – 1767), was a German soldier-engineer who became a field marshal and political figure in the Russian Empire.
155. The *Perekop* in Ukrainian: Перекоп; Russian: Перекоп; Crimean Tatar: Or Qapı; Greek: Τάφρος, is an urban-type settlement located on the Perekop Isthmus connecting the Crimean peninsula to the Ukrainian mainland. It is known for the Fortress *Or Qapi* that served as the gateway to Crimea.
156. The *Bakhchysarai* in Ukrainian: Бахчисарáй; Crimean Tatar: Bağçasaray; Russian: Бахчисарáй; Turkish: Bahçesaray; Persian: باغچه سرای, is a city in central Crimea, as well as the former capital of the Crimean Khanate.

Russians shall continue to have the right to levy hostages from the two *Kabardias*, the *Sublime Porte* being also free to levy the same for the same purpose; and in case the above-mentioned peoples of the Kabardia give ground for complaint by either of the two powers, both are permitted to punish them" (Nolde, 1953: p. 341).

Küçük Kaynarca Treaty (1774)

The next Russo-Ottoman War (1768–1774) was also an militrized crisis that fetched the *Eastern Circassia* or *Kabarda* into the Russian realm of domination. The primary resean for this armed conflict was the intricate war within the European diplomatic mechanism for an equilibrium of authority that was passable to other European states, rather than Russian dominance. Russia could have taken benefit of the tired Ottoman Empire, the end of the *Seven Years War*, and passed up France as the continent's primal martial power. The Ottoman Army losses were diplomatic in matter seeing its full reduction as a warning to Christian Europe, and the beginning of the *Eastern Question*[157] that would injure the continent until the fall of the Ottoman Empire (Schroeder, 1994, p. 35). In the Caucasian front, Russia had some troops spread out north of the Caucasus. In 1769 as a diversion, they sent *Gottlieb Heinrich Totleben*[158] south into *Georgia* and he became the first commander to have brought an organized Russian military force in *Transcaucasia* through the *Darial Gorge*[159]. This was the first time Russian troops had crossed the North Caucasus and fought in the South Caucasus with Ottomans (Avtorkhanov and Broxup, 1992: p. 73). On the steppes north of the mountains, the later-famous *Matvei Platov*[160] and 2000 men fought 25000 Ottomans and Crimeans (Mikaberidze, 2005: p.304). Finally, the Russian military under the command of Alexander Suvorov was in charge of to rout the Ottoman Army near *Kozludzha*[161] on 20 June 1774. Russia used this win to enforce Ottomans to surrender to Russia's priorities in the treaty especially about Caucasus and Circassia. A bit late, the peace treaty signed on 21 July

---

157. In diplomatic history, the "Eastern Question" refers to the strategic competition and political considerations of the European Great Powers in light of the political and economic instability in the Ottoman Empire from the late 18th to early 20th centuries. For more information, you can see: Anderson, M.S. (1966). The Eastern Question, 1774–1923: A Study in International Relations.
158. In Russian: Готлиб-Генрих Тотлебен, was a Saxon-born Russian Empire general known for his adventurism and contradictory military career during the Seven Years' War and, then, the Russo-Turkish War (1768–74) as a commander of the first Russian expeditionary force in Georgia.
159. *Darial* Gorge or pass is known Georgian Military Road in Russian.
160. Count Matvei Ivanovich Platov was a Russian general who commanded the Don Cossacks in the Napoleonic wars and founded Novocherkassk as the new capital of the Don Host Province.
161. Battle of *Kozludzha* fought on 20 June (Old Style - June 9) 1774 near the village of Kozludzha (now Suvorovo, Bulgaria) was one of the final and decisive battles of the Russo-Turkish War (1768–74).

1774, in *Küçük Kaynarca*¹⁶². The treaty was a most pejorative blow to the once-capable Ottoman sphere. It would also stop to foretell several future crises between the Ottomans and Russia. It would be only one of many efforts by Russia to take control of Ottoman lands. Because of this war, Russia could gain the Eastern Circassia or Kabarda and some part of the coastal region in the Western Circassia around the Black Sea. Ottomans ceded to Russia two key seaports, Azov and Kerch, allowing the Russian Navy and merchant fleet direct access to the Black Sea. Therefore, Russia quickly exploited *Küçük Kaynarca* for an easy excuse to go to war and take more territory from the Ottoman Empire (Schroeder, 1994).

The Kabardians reacted to this agreement by intensifying the war. The Russians also began to be more aggressive. They erected fortifications between Mozdok and Azov, under the guidance of *Alexander Suvorov*¹⁶³. The number of fortresses was established and settled by *Volga Cossacks* in 1777-1780. The Kabardians, in alliance with other North Caucasian peoples, began to display some military activities in the spring of 1779. Nearly all of the Northern Caucasus, except South Dagestan, was involved in this struggle. At the end of September 1779, the bloodiest of all battles were fought between the Kabardians and the Russian forces. Taken unawares, most of the Kabardians perished. About 50 princes and over 350 nobles fell in this battle, refusing to surrender (Namitok, 1956: p. 17).

Jassy Treaty (1792)

The War (1787–1792) involved an unsuccessful effort by the Ottoman Empire to regain territories lost to the Russian Empire in the course of the previous Russo-Ottoman War (1768–1774). The Treaty of Jassy, signed at *Jassy*¹⁶⁴ city, was affirming Russian increasing authority in the Black Sea (Hitchens, 2012, p. 20). Accordingly, the Treaty of Jassy, the *Dniester* was made the Russian frontier in Europe, while *the Russian Asiatic frontier* - the Kuban River - carried on unchanged (Sicker, 2001: p. 82). The War geographically did not take place in Circassia and the Caucasus but consequently, in the next decades, caused the Russian Imperial Army to have easier conquer in the southern Kuban River and pressurized the front military line toward Circassia.

After the *Porte*'s unsuccessful war and the conclusion of peace in Jassy on December 29, 1791, the situation of *Kabarda* and of *Circassia* in general

---

162. Today *Kaynardzha* in Bulgaria.
163. Alexander Vasilyevich Suvorov in Russian: Алекса́ндр Васи́льевич Суво́ров; 1730-1800) was a Russian military leader, considered a national hero for Russians.
164. Alternatively, *Iasi* in old Moldavia and presently in Romania.

worsened. *Catherine the Great*, made a humane gesture in disapproving the action of *General Ivan Gudovich*[165]. Commander of the Caucasian army, who had compelled some Circassian tribes to swear the oath of allegiance as Russian subjects. She told them that she released them from this oath and had "ordered them to be accepted as free peoples, dependent on no one" (Dubrovin, 1986: p. 276). She sent a letter to *Gudovich* in 1792 with this text: "It is not only by force of arms that you should conquer people who live in inaccessible mountains and who have safe shelters there from our troops, but rather through justice that you should win their trust in you, and through mildness that you should assuage bitterness, win hearts, and teach them how to behave toward Russians" (Ibid: p. 293), but this did not prevent the Russians from continuing to use force of arms. The building of fortresses on the line and in the upper reaches of the *Kuban* continued. The break in communications between Eastern and Western Circassia became permanent and the *Black Sea Cossacks* were been inhabited on *Taman peninsula* by 1792.

Bucharest Treaty (1812)

According to this Treaty[166], the Ottoman Empire conceded the eastern half of *Moldavia* to Russia, in spite of the fact that *Moldavia* was supposed to be guarded (Robarts, 2008: p. 94). This caused Russia as new player in the Danube area with the militarily, economically, diplomatically, and beneficial frontier. In *Transcaucasia*, the Ottomans refused to abide by its demands to the most of western Georgia but kept the control of *Akhalkalaki*[167], *Poti*[168], and *Anapa* which previously captured by the *Russo-Georgian troops*, therefore still some part of Western Circassia remained under the Ottoman's domain (Baddeley, 1908: Chapter.V). Actually, in every advocacy and defense of the Ottoman Empire in the Caucasus, Anapa fortress played a key role in the military plans. Therefore, to support the fortress from the Russian attack, Circassians participated in the Russo-Ottoman wars in the side of the Ottomans (Esadze, 1993: pp. 17, 26, 28).

---

165. Count Ivan Vasilyevich Gudovich in Russian: Иван Васильевич Гудович; (1741–1820) was a Russian noble and military leader of Ukrainian descent. His exploits included the capture of Hadji Bey (1789) and the conquest of maritime Dagestan (1807).
166. The treaty was approved by Alexander I of Russia on June 11, just 13 days before Napoleon's invasion of Russia commenced, that allowed many of the Russian soldiers in the Balkans to be brought back to in time for the expected attack of Napoleon.
167. *Akhalkalaki* is a town in Georgia's southern region of Samtskhe-Javakheti where most of inhabitants are Aemnians.
168. Poti is a port city in Georgia, located on the eastern Black Sea coast in the region of Samegrelo-Zemo Svaneti in the west of the country.

Adrianople Treaty (1829)

The Treaty of Adrianople[169] gave Russia, the most eastern shore of the *Black Sea* and the *Danube* area which singed on 14 September 1829. The treaty was the result of The Russo-Ottoman War (1828–1829) which was sparked by the Greek War of Independence[170] (Acton, 1907: p. 202). Although the main fighting was in the west of Caucasus front. *Paskevich*[171]'s main aims were to tie down as many Ottoman troops as possible, to take back the Ottoman forts on the Black Sea coast that supported the Circassians and might be used to soil forces, and to push the western boundary to some favorable point. At the end of this battle, Ottomans recognized Russian domination and sovereignty over the Western Caucasus. Actually, the *Sultan* recognized Russian possession of *Georgia* with *Poti, Imeretia, Mingrelia, Guria* till the fortresses of *Akhaltsikhe* and *Akhalkalaki* and even control of *Anapa* in Circassia (Tucker, 2010: p.1154). Therefore, given its events of the previous year when the *Khanates* of *Yerevan* and *Nakhichevan* had been ceded by Persia to Russia with coagulation of *Turkmenchay Treaty*[172], Russia managed to dominate almost the entire South Caucasus by 1829. It should be noted when the Ottoman Empire abandoned all its rights to the Circassian coast by this treaty, the Russo-Circassian War entered to the new phase from 1830 till the final defeat of Circassians in 1864.

After the end of the War, the Ottoman Empire relinquished North Caucasus to Russia and the Russian Empire began her military operations in order to really submit her new "subjects". In response to it the Abadzekhs, Shapsugs, Ubykhs and other Circassian tribes convened "National Allegiance Convention"[173] in 1830 and united their efforts against the Russian aggression. The continuing escalation of the Russian military operations in Circassia compelled the National Allegiance Convention to send an appeal "The Declaration of Independence of Circassia" to other governments.

---

169. Also called the Treaty of *Edirne*.
170. Also known as the *Greek Revolution* was a successful war of independence waged by Greek revolutionaries against the Ottoman Empire between 1821 and 1832.
171. Ivan Fyodorovich Paskevich in Russian: Ива́н Фёдорович Паске́вич (1782 – 1856) was an imperial Russian military leader. For his victories, he was made Count of Yerevan in 1828 and Namestnik of the Kingdom of Poland in 1831.
172. The Treaty of *Turkmenchay* was an agreement between Persia and the Russian Empire, which concluded the Russo-Persian War (1826–28). By the treaty, Persia ceded to Russia control of several areas in the South Caucasus: the Erivan Khanate, the Nakhchivan Khanate, and the remainder of the Talysh Khanate. The boundary between Russian and Persia was set at the Aras River. These territories comprise modern-day Armenia, the southern parts of the modern-day Republic of Azerbaijan, Nakhchivan, as well as Iğdır Province (now part of Turkey).
173. In Circassian: Лэпкъ Тхьэрыӏо Хасэ

Crimean War (1853 - 1856) & Paris Treaty (1856)

The Crimean War was an armed conflict struggled from October 1853 to February 1856 in which the Russian Empire lost to an alliance of the Ottoman Empire, Britain, France, and Sardinia. It was one of the greatest battles of *European History*. In addition, this war was one of the first conflicts to use pioneer and modern technologies of that time such as explosive naval shells, telegraphs, and railways (Figure. 09) (Royle, 2000).

In the end, the Treaty of Paris of 1856 appointed the Crimean War between the Russian Empire and an alliance of the Ottoman Empire, the Second French Empire, the Kingdom of Sardinia, and the British Empire (Albin, 1912: pp. 170-180). The treaty, at the *Congress of Paris* signed on 30 March 1856, caused the Black Sea impartial territory, closing it to all warships, and prohibited fortifications and the presence of armaments on its shores. The situations for the return of *Sevastopol* and other towns in the south of *Crimea* were clear; "not to establish any naval or military arsenal on the Black Sea coast". It was actually the sign of the ultimate defeat of the Ottoman military in the Caucasian front. During the process of the signature of the *Treaty of Paris*, *Sefer Bey Zanuko*[174] insisted on preparation and a provision, which would put Circassia under the Ottoman suzerainty. However, the Circassian Question was not on the agenda of the Ottoman delegation in Paris (Polovinkina: p. 143). This war was the last chance for Circassian to stay independent, however, after the treaty, even the Caucasian war got finished and Russians captured all Caucasus.

Caucasian War

After destroying the Golden Horde at the end of the 16th century and the emergence of a geographic gap, Russia began to push south toward the northern steppes of the Caucasus in a process of gradual encroachments. As time went on, several Caucasian principalities retracted southwards towards the mountains. After several retreats, Russia gained access to Persian and Ottoman-dominated areas (Jaimoukha, 2001, p. 58). This process lasted for almost a century and was accompanied by successive wars and resistance of Caucasian peoples against Russians, which it is called the *Caucasian War*[175]. This series battles and resistances historically counted from 1763 until 1864 as an invasion of the

---

174. He was a Circassian nobleman and independence activist. He took part in the various stages of the Russo-Circassian War in both a military and a political capacity. For more information, you can see: Khoon, Yahya (2015). Prince of Circassia: Sefer Bey Zanuko and the Circassian Struggle for Independence". Journal of Caucasian Studies. V.1 (1): 69–92.
175. In Russian: Кавказская война *Kavkazskaya vojna*

Caucasus by the *Russian Imperial Army*[176], which resulted in Russia's annexation of the areas of the North Caucasus (King, 2008). In the local resources, especially those who were *Muslims*, these resistances were described as *Jihad*[177] or *Holy Wars* (Kemper, 2010).

There is a special point in this war when Russian could have controlled of the *Georgian Military Highway*[178] in the center of Caucasus and then it made to divide the Caucasian War into two geographic part; first the Russo-Circassian War in the west and second, the *Murid War*[179] in the east. Actually, the war in the Northeast Caucasus, which is more popular and widely known with its *Holy War* or *Jihad* and especially with its legendary leader *Sheikh Shamil*[180], took place simultaneously and with many parallels with the war in Circassia. However, the nature of the resistance in the Northeast Caucasus was radically different from the war in *Circassia* (Dowling, 2014, pp. 728–730). Islam was still insufficiently established in *Circassia* during the wars, therefore it did not shape as a Holy War like eastern part. On the other hand, there had always been *Sufi* groups in the eastern part, especially in *Dagestan* and *Chechnya* including *Naqshbandi*[181] and *Qadiriyya*[182] orders were noted for their strict adherence to religious law[183] and the duty of a *Murid* or disciple to his teacher or *Murshid*. Howsoever, this was sincerely spiritual, under Russian push it became merged with the notion of *Gazivat*[184] and *Jihad* or *Holy War*. The ideas of religious duty, subordination and obedience to a master, tough and strict religious law and *Holy*

---

176. In Russian: Рýсская импера́торская а́рмия *ruskaya imperatorskaya armiya*
177. Jihad in English: /dʒɪˈhɑːd/; in جهاد *jihād*, is an Arabic word which literally means striving or struggling, especially with a praiseworthy aim.
178. Georgian Military Road in Russian: Военно-Грузинская дорога *Voyenno-Gruzinskaya doroga*, is the historic name for a major route through the Caucasus from Georgia to Russia. Geographically, it is called *Darial Gorge* or pass.
179. The Murid War (1829–1859) also known as the Russian Conquest of Chechnya and Dagestan was the eastern phase of the Caucasian War in which Russia conquered the independent peoples of the Caucasus Mountains.
180. He was an Avar political and religious leader of the Muslims of the Northern Caucasus. He was a leader of anti-Russian resistance in the Caucasian War and was the third Imam of the Caucasian Imamate (1840–1859).
181. The *Naqshbandi* or *Naqshbandiyah* in Arabic: نقشبندية is a major Sunni spiritual order of Sufism. It got its name from Baha-ud-Din Naqshband Bukhari and traces its spiritual lineage to the Islamic prophet Muhammad, through Abu Bakr, the first Caliph and Muhammad's companion. Some Naqshbandi masters trace their lineage through Ali his son-in-law and successor, in keeping with most other Sufis. For more information, you can see: Itzchak Weismann (2007). The Naqshbandiyya: Orthodoxy and Activism in a Worldwide Sufi Tradition. Routledge.
182. The *Qadiriyya* in Arabic: القادرية, are members of the Qadiri tariqa (Sufi order). The tariqa got its name from Abdul Qadir Gilani (1077–1166, also transliterated Jilani), who was from Gilan. The order relies strongly upon adherence to the fundamentals of Islam. For more information, you can see: Abun-Nasr, Jamil M. "The Special Sufi Paths (Taqiras)", in Muslim Communities of Grace: The Sufi Brotherhoods in Islamic Religious Life. New York: Columbia UP, 2007. 86–96.
183. *Sharia* law, or Islamic law (Arabic: شريعة) is the religious law forming part of the Islamic tradition.
184. Or *Ghazi* (غازي, ġāzī) is an Arabic term originally referring to an individual who participates in ghazw (غزو, ġazw), meaning military expeditions or raiding; after the emergence of Islam, it took on new connotations of religious warfare. The related word *ghazwa* (غزوة ġazwah) is a singulative form meaning a battle or military expedition, often one led by the Islamic prophet Muhammad.

War became the base of an armed-theocratic state that opposed the massive Russian Empire for thirty years. The religion was an important factor for holding together the many independent villages, families, and clans, but it should be noted that the Circassians held out even longer without the help of a theocratic state. *Moshe Gammer* (1994) in his book 'Muslim Resistance to the Tsar' gives a complex account of the religious origin of the movement, which will not be reproduced here. In addition, I should mention that this war was the first attempt for both eastern and western parts to make their identities through a new phenomenon, which I mean Russians in their territories.

In summary, the main part of the war was accomplished during the reigns of three successive *Russian Tsars*: *Alexander I* (1801–1825), *Nicholas I* (1825–1855), and *Alexander II* (1855–1881). The outstanding Russian commanders were included *Aleksey Petrovich Yermolov*[185] in 1816–1827, *Mikhail Semyonovich Vorontsov* in 1844–1853, and *Aleksandr Baryatinskiy* in 1853–1856.

The first period of the invasion terminated coincidentally with the death of Alexander I and the *Decembrist Revolt* in 1825. It attained amazingly little success, especially compared with the recent Russian victory over the *Great Army of Napoleon* (1812). Between 1825 and 1833, little military activities happened in the Caucasus against the North Caucasians indigenous as wars with Ottoman (1828-1829) and with Persian (1826-1828) occupied the Russians. After significant achievements in both wars, Russia resumed attacking the Caucasus against the several rebelling local ethnic groups in the North Caucasus. Russian units again met resistance, notably led by *Imam Qazi Mullah*[186], *Imam Gamzat-bek*[187], *Hadji Murad*[188], *Sheikh Mansur*[189], and *Imam Shamil*.

The Eastern part war ended in 1859; the Russians could capture *Imam Shamil*, forced him to surrender and crumble, to swear faithfulness to the *Tsar*, and then banished him to Central Russia. Afterward, having gained achievement in the east, Russian forces removed remaining opposition in the west during the next several years. Ultimately, as many as Circassians in the west, were relocated

---

185. Aleksey Petrovich Yermolov in Russian: Алексе́й Петро́вич Ермо́лов, (1777 – 1861) was a Russian Imperial general of the 19th century who commanded Russian troops in the Caucasian War.
186. Or *Imam Ghazi Muhammad* as an Islamic scholar and ascetic, who was the first Imam of the Caucasian Imamate (from 1828 to 1832).
187. Or *Hamza-Bek ibn Ali Iskandar Bek al-Hutsali* (1789-1834) was the second imam of the Caucasian Imamate, who succeeded Ghazi Mollah upon his death in 1832.
188. *Hadji Murad* in Russian: Хаджи-Мурат, was an important Avar leader during the Caucasian resistance in Dagestan and Chechnya in 1811–1864.
189. Also known as *Sheikh al-Mansur*, was a Chechen Islamic religious and military leader who led the resistance against Catherine the Great's imperialist expansion into the Caucasus. He remains a hero of the Chechen people and its struggle for independence.

from their ancestral lands. As respects, the war in the Western part resumed with the Circassians renovating the battle. A statement of *Tsar Alexander II* declared the end of hostilities on June 2, 1864 (Derluguian, 2009) (Map. 16).

Murid War

The main part of *Murid War* held between 1829 until 1859 which it calls the Russian Conquest of Chechnya and Dagestan in the eastern phase of the *Caucasian War*. Later, the *Dagestani* and *Chechen* tribes joined in the *Caucasian Imamate*[190], a military-theocratic state that held out for thirty years. This new local state was created by *Ghazi Muhammad* in 1829–1832 and governed by *Imam Shamil* from 1834 until his submission in 1859. It should be noted that before *Murid War*, there were some resistance in the eastern of Caucasus that I do not count it under this war, specifically by *Sheikh Mansur* (1760–1794) who was a *Chechen* Islamic religious and military leader that led the resistance against *Catherine the Great*'s imperialist expansion into the Caucasus during the late 18th century.

After establishing control over the Southern Caucasus as discussed above, Russia headed for the North Caucasus, a region that had long stood firm against invasion. While *East North Caucasians* actively resisted the Russians, when *Sheikh Shamil*'s forces finally succumbed to the Russians. There are several reasons for *Sheikh Shamil*'s defeat. First of all, he only could assemble the central and eastern parts of the North Caucasus. Circassians in the western region of the North Caucasus were worn out after their own lengthy battles against *Russian Tsar*. Additionally, the Circassians did not view the political regime of Imamate applied by Chechen and Dagestani as rightful and legitimate. (Gafarli, 2014: pp. 172-175)

With the end of the *Crimean War* in 1856, Russia was free to turn its full attention to the Caucasus. On 22 July 1856, *Prince Aleksandr Baryatinsky*[191] was appointed both *Viceroy* and commander-in-chief and set about reorganizing the armies. Earlier, from 1848 to 1856 he took a leading part in all the chief military events in the Caucasus, his most notable exploits being his operations against *Shamil* in *Chechnya*. The general plan for the future was for the northern army to move southeast through *Chechnya* and link up with the *Dagestan* army

---

190. The Caucasian Imamate, also known as the Caucasus Imamate in Arabic: إمامة القوقاز `Imāmat al-Qawqāz, was the state established by the imams in Dagestan and Chechnya during the early-to-mid 19th century in the Northern Caucasus, to fight against the Russian Empire during the Caucasian War, where Russia sought to conquer the Caucasus in order to secure communications with its new territories south of the mountains.
191. Aleksandr Ivanovich Baryatinsky in Russian: Александр Иванович Барятинский; (1815 - 1879) was a Russian General and Field Marshal (from 1859), Prince, governor of the Caucasus.

in the alley of the *Andi Koysu*[192] while the southern army moved northward (Chisholm, 1911: pp. 455-456).

Shamil also was well known in particular for his capture of two princesses in 1854. He was defeated in 1861. A bold warrior, he would not have been defeated if the *Crimean war* (1853-1856) had not freed the Russians' hand to bring the full force of their army to bear on the uprising in the Caucasus.

Actually, *Murid* is a follower of a *Shaykh*[193] and had the two lives in a *Khaniqah*[194] or monastery and lead a very austere existence. Finally, the *Shaykh* leads the *Murid* on the direction of *Tariqa*[195]. The term *'Murid'* is also used for an individual who fights voluntarily for social equality and for national independence. In this context, *Muridism* is accepted as a chapter of *Sufism* in which the apprentice follows the orders of an *Imam* who leads the *Ghazavat* or *Holy War* for equality and public integrity (Figure. 10).

Caucasian Military Line

The Caucasian Military Line or in some sources *'Caucasus Line Cossack Host'* and 'The North Caucasus Line' was a line of Russian forts and Cossack settlements along the north side of the Caucasus which were originating from 16th century with a few free Cossacks near the Caspian Sea, to the 19th century when the line was pushed west and used as a basis to gain the southern mountains and to occupy the northen steppes. Actually, it was a military line created officially in 1832 for the purpose of the army conquest. This line had an important role in the conquest during the Caucasian War and even as a reason for the beginning of the war.

When the first military outpost in Circassia was established in 1763 on the left bank of Terek River, Kabardians entered into negotiations with Russians and they sent their emissary Qeisin Qeitoqwe[196] to Saint Petersburg to protest the foundation of the fort. He presented a petition in which the limits of Kabardian Lands or Eastern Circassia as conceived by the inhabitants themselves were recorded: "The Kabardian lands extended, on one part, to the River Kuma and ruins of the ancient town of Madjar and on the part down the Terek River until

---

192. The Andi-Koysu in Russian: Андийское Койсу - Andiyskoye Koysu, in Georgian: ანდის ყოისუ - Andis Qoisu) is a river and valley in Georgia and Dagestan.
193. Sheikh is an honorific title in the Arabic language.
194. Khaniqah in Persian: خانقاه, is a building designed specifically for gatherings of a Sufi brotherhood or tariqa and is a place for spiritual retreat and character reformation.
195. A tariqa in Arabic: طريقة *ṭarīqah*, is a school or order of Sufism, or specifically a concept for the mystical teaching and spiritual practices of such an order with the aim of seeking Haqiqa, which translates as "ultimate truth".
196. In Cricassian: Къетыкъуэ Къесын

the locality of Meken on the said river at least 60 verts down river from Mozdok" (Nolde, 1953: p. 344). Therefore, I think it was the first reaction of Circassian to a new phenomenon in the region and beginning of Circassian Question in the history of Caucasus. This act may be regarded as a flagrant contravention of article six of the treaty of Belgrade. By 1769, a line of fortifications was extended eastwards to Kizlyar, followed by a string of fortresses in the opposite direction that extended northwestwards to the Azov Sea, forming the so-called the Caucasian Military Line. The Line was completed in 1832, cutting off contact between the Circassians and Ottomans also along the Black Sea coast (Jaimoukha, 2001: pp. 59-60) (Map. 16-17).

Russo - Circassian War

The Russo-Circassian War as it is mentioned above refers to a series of battles from 1763 until 1864 in Circassia and it counts as western part of Caucasian War. I used the term Russo-Circassian War, its starting date as 1763, when the Russians began establishing forts, including at *Mozdok*, to be used as the primary frontier for conquest toward Circassia (Henze, 1992: p. 266) and settling down of Cossacks there. Additionally, I used the end of the war as the signing of loyalty oaths by Circassian leaders on 2 June 1864[197]. Afterward, the Ottoman Empire offered to refuge the Circassians that did not wish to accept the rule of a Christian monarch and Russian Empire, therefore many emigrated to Ottoman lands (Shenfield, 1999: pp. 149-162).

According to the pre-Soviet historians, this war hanged on for a long-term, almost for two hundred years. There are other historians, who are asserting that this war started sharply in 1817. It has come from A. A. *Gaspari*'s idea, who had first settled this point of view, in 1904. They tried to knit the beginning of *General Aleksey Petrovich Yermolov*'s military campaign to the Caucasus. The enormous plurality of the historians, however, came to the termination that 'The Russo-Caucasian War' started in 1763 and remained until 1864 (Natho, 2009: p. 267).

The war did not have a clear beginning. Instead of fighting slowly increased as more and more Russians moved south. From 1777, the Russians constructed a line of the fortresses from Mozdok to the northwest toward the Azov Sea. Before 1800 the main Russian push was on the Kabardians near the southeast end of this crosswise. The first castle emerged along the western Kuban river in 1778. During the Russo-Ottoman War (1787–92) the Russians made three

---

197. Some sources: 21 may

attempts to take Anapa by crossing Circassian territory. The second effort was a tragedy when the Circassians harried the Russians going and coming. The Kuban Line took its fundamental figure in 1792-93. *Black Sea Cossacks*[198] were settled north of the lower *Kuban* in 1792/93 and *Don Cossacks* on the *Kuban* bend in 1794.

Actually, Russian pressure increased in the Caucasus after a relaxation of the European front with the signing of the *Treaty of Versailles* in 1763. Once *Catherine the Great* decided to invade the northeastern shores of the *Black Sea* in the 1760s, the Russian military worked to expel Circassians from the region bit-by-bit until they were surrounded in the high mountains (Richmond, 2013: p. 08). After the second war between Russia and the Ottoman Empire in 1768, the Ottomans were forced to cede Crimea and the North Caucasus to Russia after the Treaty of Küçük Kaynarca in 1774. In 1779, Empress Catherine instructed the Governor General of Astrakhan, Prince Potemkin, to pacify Kabardia by fair means or foul. After the Kabardian Army was defeated by Russian forces in 1779, Russian rule began to take root in Kabarda. The situation became worse when Russian troops occupied the *Kuban* in 1781 and *Crimea* in 1784 (Jaimoukha, 2001: p. 61) (Map. 02).

By 1801, the Russians reduced Georgia to a protectorate and formed a vice around the North Caucasus tribes, which sealed the fate of Circassians. Eventually, Russia increased its authority in the region, and in 1810 conducted a campaign in which many Circassians were killed, and approximately 200 Circassian villages were burned (Ibid: p. 62).

Not only Circassia, but also North Caucasus, and the entire Caucasus continued to be the arena of an acute contest between the Ottoman and Russian Empires for a long time. Because of this contest, the Circassians and other mountaineers became gradually cut off from the outside world, which has considerably deteriorated their situation. We should remember here that, as a part of this plan, Russia had masterfully cut off the eastern Circassia or '*Kabarda*' from the Western Circassia as early as in 1822 (King, 2008: p. 96).

The title of the great Prince of *Kabarda* was abolished in 1822, and Russian pressure in the region increased through 1825. During this time, many Kabardians immigrated to the western Caucasus and continued their war against Russian forces. Although Russian forces subjugated *Kabarda*, *Kabardians* searched for allies to continue their fight instead of accepting defeat.

From 1840, *Imam Shamil* tried to organize a unity among all Circassians in the North Caucasus. On one hand, he attacked Russian forces on the western front; on the other hand, he sent envoys to the *Kabardians* to organize unity in

---

198. former Zaporozians

the region. However, effective cooperation between the two flanks of the North Caucasus was never obtained. The Russians were aware of Circassian indifference to Sufism and the disinclination of many of them to join forces with *Shamil* to organize unified attacks. Therefore, Russians lived in the luxury of being able to concentrate their attacks on one front without compromising their position on the other. The *Crimean War* of 1853–1856 created great hope for Circassians that Western powers, especially England, would intervene on their behalf and deliver them from the claws of Russia. The expectation reached its peak after the Russian defeat; however, at the negotiations, Russians managed to buy off the Ottomans and secure a free hand in the Northwest Caucasus. The fate of the North Caucasus was entrusted to the delicate care of Russians with the approval of the Western Powers. The only gain for Circassians from the Crimean War was that they were spared Russian aggression for three years, while Russia turned to vengeance on the Mountaineers, whose morale had reached its nadir (Jaimoukha, 2001: p. 67). The flight from the Caucasus started during the 1820s on a small scale and gained speed during the early 1860s. A campaign of *Russification*[199] and Christianization began in 1843 when the 'Caucasus Spiritual Consistory' was created in Stavropol and started to sever the cultural and religious ties of the region with the Ottomans (Richmond, 2013: p.139). Within the atmosphere of Russian pressure, Circassians had no chance to flee "to escape the forced sedentarization and Christianization[200] programs of Tsarist Russia" (Avagyan, 2004: p. 32). Immigration reached its peak during the mid-1860s after Russia issued a decree commanding Circassians to abandon their homelands. In 1859, after a bitter guerilla war that lasted thirty years, *Shamil* surrendered after the capture of the mountainous stronghold of Gunib[201] (Jaimoukha, 2001: p. 67). After this cessation, Russian forces in *Chechnya* turned westward. In 1861, the western tribes of the Caucasus organized a national meeting in Sochi to construct a civilian administration to fight against Russian forces. The final pacification of the Northern Caucasus and the great exodus of locals came in 1864. Finally, Russia was able to crush eastern Circassians in 1859, and then the western Circassians in 1864 (Ibid: p. 66).

---

199. *Russification* (Russian: Русификация), or Russianization, is a form of cultural assimilation process during which non-Russian communities, voluntarily or not, give up their culture and language in favor of the Russian one. For more information, you can see: Weeks, Theodore R. (2004). Russification: Word and Practice 1863–1914. Proceedings of the American Philosophical Society. 148 (4): 471–489. (Online access: https://web.archive.org/web/20120523232533/http://www.amphilsoc.org/sites/default/files/480407.pdf)
200. Christianization (or Christianisation) is the conversion of individuals to Christianity or the conversion of entire groups at once. Various strategies and techniques were employed in Christianization campaigns from Late Antiquity and throughout the Middle Ages in Russia.
201. In Russian: Гуниб, is a rural locality and the administrative center of Gunibsky District of the Republic of Dagestan, Russia.

Generally, the *Russo - Circassian War* can be divided into two phases. The first phase of the Russo - Circassian War was the battle, which took place in Eastern Circassia, *Kabarda*. Only after the Eastern Circassia, was annexed, the war moved to the western part. The first battle between the Russians and the Kabardians happened near the Malka River in 1771, which eventuated by Russian victory. The bloodiest struggle was fought in 1779, and almost 50 princes and 350 nobles died. The *Kabardians* tried to find the protection of the *Porte* and attached against Russians during the *Russo-Ottoman wars* of 1787-1791, and 1806-1812. *General Yermolov*, the military commander of the southern Russian forces, arrived in the region in 1816. *Yermolov* requested that the mountainous Kabardians move in the plains to comfort their control. Then, the Caucasian military line was pushed further into the Kabardian territory and many massacres were committed by the Russian forces (Ibid: pp. 60-63) (Map. 18).

Kabardian Role

The *Kabardians* established and created their first state in the 16th and 17th centuries in the center of the North Caucasus. This was only possible after the end of the Golden Horde, when a power vacancy was created by the failure of *Tokhtamysh*[202], a descendant of *Genghis Khan*[203] and last khan of the *White Horde*[204], at the hands of the mighty Tatar Tamerlane in 1395 by the Terek River. The *Kabardians* gradually reclaimed their lands in East Circassia beginning of the 15th century. Generally, the Kabardian resistance was localized and badly organized. The Circassian princes were unsuccessful to set up an allied front, and the Russians took the privilege of the internal contest. Despite their failure, the Kabardians were always looking for a foreign ally to uprise against the Russians (Kormezli, 2004: p.22).

Since *Ivan the Terrible* had married *Princess Gosheney*, Russia was inchmeal changing Kabarda and Kabardians unrecognizably and against their intention. She did that via the policy of divide and legislation; by setting the proud Kabardian princes against each other, by showering them with 'the gratuities of the Sovereign', by taking hostages from them to ensure their allegiance, and by

---

202. Tokhtamısh (died 1406), a prominent khan of the Blue Horde, briefly unified the White Horde and Blue Horde subdivisions of the Golden Horde into a single state. He descended from Genghis Khan's grandson, Tuqa-Timur.
203. 1st Khagan of the Mongol Empire
204. According to the *Tarikh-i Dost Sultan* written by *Ötemish Hajji* in *Khiva* in the 1550s, Batu's ulus was officially known as the White Horde under the category of 'Wings of the Golden Horde' after Genghis Khan's eldest son, *Jochi*.

giving to a pick few high positions in the Russian army, administration, and even in the imperial court (Natho, 2010: p. 718).

This time, the Kabardians organized the Eastern Circassia. By the XV century, the Kabardian princes had received so powerfully that they had expanded their effect and influence over all the neighboring regions. In fact, that was the main reason Ivan the Terrible had married the daughter of *Prince Temriuk Idarov* (Natho, 2009: p. 141).

The *Kabardians* maintained contacts with *Shamil* and the other Circassians. However, with the exception of the year 1846, it is not possible to mention about any armed stand of a significant dimension against Russians after *Yermolov* effectively crushed the organized Kabardian resistance. Russia was actually successful in its purposes to supply the security of *the Georgian Military Road* and to prevent a North Caucasian league by controlling Kabarda. The main *Kabardian* role began during the Russo - Ottoman Wars of 1768-74 when the Ottoman army attached the *Caucasus Military Line* in 1768 and *Kabardians*, who retained their might, attacked the town of *Kizlyar* and sacked it from Russians. After cessation of hostilities in 1774, the Ottomans ceded *Kabarda* and *Crimea* to Russia in the *Kuchuk Kaynarji Treaty*, despite that fact the Porte had no claim whatever over *Kabarda* (Hurewitz, 1975: pp. 92-101). The Russians pursued a policy of gradual annexation of northern Circassian lands by dislodging the indigenes and replacing them with the loyal Cossacks.

The position of the Kabardians became even more precarious when Russia occupied the *Kuban* in 1781 and annexed the *Crimea* in 1783. Plenty groups of Tatars, the formerly enemies, took asylum in Circassia, the Khans kept their titles. Sensing the threat posed by Russia, the Circassians and *Nogais* launched joint attacks on the Russians in the Western Caucasus in 1784, but no serious harm came out of these forays (Jaimoukha, 2001: pp. 60-63).

Consequences of Russian Conquest

Russians employed a lethal combination of numerical superiority and systematic reduction of resistance in the forested foothills and mountains after coming to the North Caucasus. In this long war of attrition, the Circassians suffered heavy losses in terms of human life, as much as 800,000 dead, and their land was destroyed. Many tribes were wiped out, notably the *Ubykh*. After the end of the war, the Russians expelled the majority of Circassians to the Ottoman Empire by pursuing a policy of organized and systematic terror. Whole villages were plundered and then burnt down. Thousands of people were killed in cold blood. Those hideous acts, together with the conspiracy of the Ottomans, terminated in a large-scale exodus that irreparably compromised the demographic equilibrium in Circassia. It is approximated that more than a million people were forced to move and only 800,000 were eventually settled in the Ottoman Empire' territory. The difference being the victims of starvation, disease, shipping accidents, and the disordered Ottoman administrative system. Those who stayed in the homeland were obligated to resettle in the northern plains of the Caucasus (Map. 19).

In the reaction to continuous Circassian resistance and the defeat of their previous course of building fortresses, the Russian army began using a strategy of disproportionate punishment for ravages. With the purpose of impressive stability and authority beyond their running line of control and over the Caucasus, Russian troops reprised by perishing villages or any place that resistance warriors were thought to fudge, moreover engaging the assassinations and hanging of warriors' families (King, 2008: pp. 47–49). Charles King, the historian, says in his book 'The Ghost of Freedom: A History of the Caucasus' as one of the most important sources of this wars: "Understanding that the resistance was reliant on being fed by sympathetic villages, the Russian military also systematically destroyed crops and livestock. These tactics further enraged natives and intensify resistance to Russian rule. The Russians began to counter this by modifying the terrain, in both the environment and the demographics. They cleared forests by roads, destroyed native villages, and often settled new farming communities of Russians or pro-Russian Caucasian peoples. In this increasingly bloody situation, the wholesale destruction became a standard action by the Russian army and Cossack units, and was adopted by Circassians and other highland groups against Russian or pro-Russian villages" (Ibid: p. 74).

However, the Circassian resistance continued. The villages that had formerly avowed Russian rule were found uprising again, much to the rage of Russian admirals. As well as, the Circassian cause started to awaken sympathies in the West, especially Britain (Ibid: pp. 93-94).

Dmitry Milyutin[205] suggested as a first commander, the idea of Circassian exile and expulsions in 1857. *Miliutin* argued that the purpose was not to simply displace them so that their fields could be settled by productive farmers from other regions, that "eliminating the Circassians was to be an end in itself - to cleanse the land of hostile elements". Tsar Alexander II supported the idea and Milyutin later promoted as the minister of war in 1861 and from the early 1860s, exile began (Ibid: p. 94).

---

205. *Count Dmitry Alekseyevich Milyutin* in Russian: Дмитрий Алексеевич Милютин (1816 – 1912), was Minister of War (1861–81) and the last Field Marshal of Imperial Russia (1898). He was responsible for sweeping military reforms that changed the face of the Russian army in the 1860s and 1870s.

Till the end of the war, the *General Yevdokimov* was tasked with driving the remained Circassians out of the Caucasus, essentially into the Ottoman Empire. This attitude was imposed by moving columns of Russian soldier and Cossack troops (Levene, 2005: p.297). "In a series of sweeping military campaigns lasting from 1860 to 1864, the northwest Caucasus and the Black Sea coast were virtually emptied of Muslim villagers. Columns of the displaced were marched either to the Kuban plains or toward the coast for transport to the Ottoman Empire. One after another, entire Circassian tribal groups were dispersed, resettled, or killed" (King, 2008: pp.94–96). Such a strategy had been used for several years.

During the Russian imperial years, *Kabarda* was classified under the *Stavropol Province*. *Cossack* and *Russian* settlers found a new place in the northeastern parts of *Kabarda*. According to the Russian sources, there were about 70,000 *Kabardians* in *Kabarda* in the early years of the 20th century (Chisholm, 1911: p. 619).

The once mighty *Kabardians* had been reduced to a subject people of Russia by the middle of the 19th century. Despite their defeat, the Kabardians were always on the lookout for an external ally to rise up against the occupiers. This expulsion, along with the actions of the Russian military in acquiring Circassia (Shenfield, 1999: p. 150), has given rise to a movement among descendants of the expelled ethnicities for international recognition that genocide was perpetrated. Some sources give us the number of hundreds of thousands died during the exile. Some historians use the course of 'Circassian massacres' for this Russian consequences in Circassia (Levene, 2005: p. 299, 302). At the same time then that Russian officials were congratulating each other on victory, lauding the glory of the Russian troops and the greatness of the Russian nation, many masses of refugees were still camping on the Black Sea coast, waiting for Ottoman ships to take them to the other part of sea. Eyewitnesses described the shores as strewn with dead bodies. Shiploads upon shiploads of starving, half-naked Circassians, further weakened by infected illness and diseases, were getting the Ottoman lands. The following report provided by a Russian who worked in the army demonstrates the savagery of the campaign in which no quarter was asked or given:

"The war proceeded with inexorable and merciless severity. We pushed ahead one step at a time, but remorselessly, clearing every patch of land where a soldier set foot on mountaineers, down to the last man. The mountain *auls* were burned by the hundred. The snow had only just melted away, but it was before the trees had become clothed in their greenery (in February and March); the crops were eaten by the horses or even trampled down. If we managed to catch the inhabitants of the *auls* unawares, they were immediately led away under military escort to the shores of the Black Sea and then sent to Turkey. How many times did it happen that in the huts which had been hurriedly abandoned upon our approach we found warm gruel with a spoon in it on the table, clothing which was being repaired and with the needle still in it, and various children's toys which looked as though they had been spread out on the floor next to a child. Sometimes very seldom, bestial atrocities were committed" (Baytugan, 1971: pp. 1-38).

Circassian historians quote the figures of near the four million marks, while official Russian figures are almost 300,000. The Russian statistics of 1897 records only 150,000 Circassians, one-tenth of the original number, remained after the war. Some Russian, Caucasian, and Western historians agree on the figure of approximately 500,000 residents of Circassia being deported by Russian by force in the 1860s. A large number of them died in transmission from the diseases and starving. Some of those that remained faithful to Russia were resettled into the plains, the left bank of the Kuban River (King, 2008: p. 96) (Table. 09).

British Connection

According to documents and travel notes, Circassia was very much attracted the interest of Britain since 1830s with the print of Portfolio, the Vixen affair and journeys of David Urquhart, James Stanislaus Bell, John Longworth, and Edmund Spencer to Circassia[206]. Definitely British efforts to encourage and support resistance in the Caucasus were almost entirely outside the margin of conventional diplomacy. They were intended to keep hopes of resistance alive, to harass a potential enemy, and to preserve options for more vigorous future action if international developments made it desirable and circumstances favored it (Henze, 1990, p. 27). In the context of the "Eastern Question", outside support for Circassian anticolonial resistance seemed a probate way for curbing Russian influence in the region. British considerations included setting up a Circassian protectorate in order to gain a foothold in the region. (Brock, 1956: p. 401-427; King, 2007: p. 238-255)

---

206. These British adventurers wrote books about the Circassian resistance and their residences in Circassia, which are so valuable for the Circassian history, while we learn many details about Circassia of that time from these books, because of the lack of written literature among the Circassians. John Longworth, A Year among Circassians (1837-38) (Two volumes) (London, 1840); J. S. Bell, Journal of a Residence in Circassia 1836, 1837, 1838 (Two volumes) (London, 1840); Edmund Spencer, Travels in Circassia, Krim-Tartary, etc. (Two volumes) (London, 1839); Captain Spencer, Turkey, Russia, the Black Sea, and Circassia (London, 1854).

In contrast to Russian negative representations, European powers like England produced a romantic image of Circassians as noble knights, heroically fighting barbarian Russia[207]. In 19th century, the British government sent missions, amongst David Urquhart[208] would be the most popular one, to the region about trade opportunities. He arrived in Istanbul from Greece in 1831 and was employed by British Ambassador Stratford Canning as a confidential aide. He had been transformed into an ardent Turcophile[209] by the time he returned to England where in 1833 he published a book entitled 'Turkey and its Resources'. This book so pleased King William IV that he sent it to all his ministers and urged his foreign minister, Henry John Temple, 3rd Viscount Palmerston[210], to make future use of the young activist author (Henze, 1990: p. 30). Actually, Near Eastern countries were providing a huge market for the British goods. Not only the trade with the Ottoman Empire, but also the trade with Persia, the Caucasus, and even Russia was considered and evaluated in the foreign policy circles of Britain (Luxenburg, 1998: p. 142). On the other hand, it was obvious that British goods would not drive into the territories under the Russian rule as easy as it entered into a territory under the British influence (Gleason, 1950: p. 170).

By the end of 1837, Russophobia[211] was a major part of the English opinion, for which David Urquhart was mostly responsible. David Urquhart's visit to Circassia in 1834 was important for the future British involvements in Circassia. He had a mission to research the resources of Ottomans, especially those which could be bought from Anatolia instead of Russia (Luxenburg, 1998: p. 92).

Encouraged by Lord Ponsonby, the new British Ambassador in Istanbul, Urquhart started a journey on the Black Sea. During his visit to Samsun, Urquhart met Sefer Bey Zanuko[212] (Figure. 11) who was at that time organizing

---

207. See for more example: Bell, James: Journal of a Residence in Circassia during the Years 1837, 1838, and 1839, London 1840; Lapinski, Theophil: Die Bergvölker des Kaukasus und ihr Freiheitskampf gegen die Russen. Hamburg 1863.
208. David Urquhart was a Scot, an ardent Turcophil and an expert of the Near Eastern matters. After his visit to the Caucasus in 1834, he acted as an advocate and spokesperson of the Caucasians in the West. He was admired and backed by Sir Herbert Taylor, the King's private secretary, and his writings greatly appreciated by the King William IV. He published the polemical journal Portfolio, and wrote several books about the importance of the Ottoman Empire and the Caucasus, as well as the Russian threat against the British interests. Gleason, p. 146.
209. Turcophile (comparative more Turcophile, superlative most Turcophile) Favouring or sympathetic to Turkey.
210. He was a British statesman who served twice as Prime Minister in the mid-19th century. Palmerston dominated British foreign policy during the period 1830 to 1865, when Britain was at the height of her imperial power.
211. Anti-Russian sentiment or Russophobia is a diverse spectrum of negative feelings, dislikes, fears, aversion, derision and/or prejudice of Russia, Russians or Russian culture. A wide variety of mass culture clichés about Russia and Russians exists.
212. He was a Circassian nobleman and independence activist. He took part in the various stages of the Russo-Circassian War in both a military and a political capacity. Advocating for the cause of Circassian independence in the west and acting as an emissary of the Ottoman Empire in the region. By the end of his life, Zanuko had emerged as the leader of the Circassian independence movement.

"the illegal trade" between Anatolia and Circassia. It should be noted that the most prominent Circassian with whom Urquhart and all other Englishmen were in contact in Constantinople was Sefer Bey who had gone to Anatolia as representative of the confederated Circassian Princes to organize support for Circassian resistance during the Russo - Circassian Wars (Bell, 2007: Vol I, pp. 267-71). While Urquhart visited Circassia with reference letters of Sefer Bey, shortly after this meeting Sefer Bey went to Istanbul to get the support of the European powers for the Circassian cause. His residence in the British Embassy in Istanbul demonstrated his close relations with the British diplomatic circles[213].

In the summer of 1834, Urquhart visited Circassia where he received a petition signed by 11 chiefs requesting the British king to intervene into the conflict. Two more petitions followed in 1835 and 1836 respectively, both were reluctantly rejected by the British ambassador in Constantinople John Ponsonby, 1st Viscount Ponsonby[214]. Lord Palmerston had previously blocked Ponsonby's initiative to include Circassia in the Eastern Question, because of the feeble state of the Circassian resistance movement. A series of diplomatic protests by the Russian ambassador led to Zanuko's exile to Edirne. Encouraged by Urquhart a group of British adventurers unsuccessfully attempted to run the blockade of the Circassian coast, the Mission of the Vixen created a diplomatic scandal between Britain and Russia. Encouraged by Ponsonby, Zanuko continued to submit appeals to the British albeit to no avail (Köremezli, 2004: pp. 26-36) (Map. 20). In 1836, he dispatched a British schooner that was filled with arms illegally bound for Circassian resistance forces. Russian forces seized the "Vixen" after it attempted to run a naval blockade and land its cargo on the Circassian coastline. The "Vixen Incident"[215], the result of a lone diplomat's unsupported desire to help the Circassians, nearly caused a war between Britain and Russia (Hopkirk, 2001: pp. 158-159).

Lord Ponsonby wrote to the Foreign Ministry that it was time to support the Circassians, as he thought that the Circassian war was a part of the Eastern Question and the balance of powers (Luxenburg, 1998: p. 96). In one of his reports, Ponsonby stated that he had sent a message to Circassia about the establishment of a government and the announcement of an independence declaration (Ibid: p. 98). He also pointed out that the invasion of the Caucasus would yield more power to Russia than the suppression of Poland (Ibid: p. 100).

---

213. You can see more details: "From Baron Wrangel to Baron Rosen, 16 [28] August 1835", AKAK, Vol. VIII, p. 890; "From Baron Rosen to Graf Nesselrode, 31 October [12 November] 1835", AKAK, Vol. VIII, pp. 891-892.
214. John Ponsonby, 1st Viscount Ponsonby, GCB (1770 – 22 February 1855) was a longtime British diplomat and politician.
215. In British history, named "The mission of the Vixen"

However, the Foreign Ministry refused Ponsonby's claims on the necessity of rendering support to Circassia (Ibid: p. 101).

Besides the activities of Sefer Bey, another matter that bothered the Russian government was the British adventurers in the Caucasus. After the arrival of James Bell and John Longworth, Raevskiy also reported about the alleged British agents of, Marrin and Iddo, who came to Circassia with two ships full of arms. According to this report, Captain Marrin and the Polish Polinsky swore to return the Caucasus again with Longworth[216]. The fact that those adventurers were not prevented, if not encouraged, by the British government to act in Circassia promoted the belief in Russia that they were the agents of the British government. However, the British Government and the Foreign Office were very careful in their actions and attitudes towards Russia. Nonetheless, the anti-Russian circles in Britain, which also enjoyed the sympathy of the King William IV, fostered the Russian anxiety that the British Foreign Office was intervening in Russia's internal matters. The British ambassadors in Istanbul also harbored similar views to those of the Russophobic society in Britain. Ponsonby and Stratford Canning enjoyed not only special influence and respect in Ottoman, but at the same time, they had undeniable pro-Ottoman and anti-Russian tendencies (Temperley, 1964: pp. 74-75). They thought that the profits of Britain lied in the protection of the well-being of the Ottoman Empire, and the prevention of the future Russian expansion. In this context, the independence of Circassia was essential to prevent the Russian advance (Ibid: pp. 75-76). Actually, during this period, it seems that Ponsonby and Urquhart supported a more active policy for the protection of the Indian route. They believed that, if Circassia fell, then the Ottoman lands would come to the fore. Therefore, not only the Russian expansion should be prevented, but also a powerful Ottoman should be restored for the future benefits of Britain.

There is much still to be learned about foreign interest in, and involvement with, the Circassian resistance struggle. Ottoman archives should eventually broaden our understanding (Saray, 1988). Both Ottoman and British states were intended to keep hopes of resistance alive, harass a potential enemy, and preserve options for more vigorous future action if international developments made it desirable and circumstances favored it. Among Ottoman officialdom there were many who abetted what their countrymen were doing to help the Circassians. However, neither Palmerston expressed in a letter to Lord John Russell during the Crimean War are probably not far from those he held in the 1830s:

---

216. You can see more details: Report from General-adjutant Lazarev to Baron Rosen, 24 November [6 December] 1837, AKAK, Vol. VIII; "From Golovin to Chernyshev", AKAK, Vol. IX, p. 453.

"To expel the Russians from the Danubian principalities and leave them in full strength would only be like turning a burglar out of your house, to break in again at more fitting opportunities. The best and most effectual security for the future peace of Europe would be the severance from Russia of some of the frontier territories acquired by her in later times, Georgia, Circassia, the Crimea, Bessarabia, Poland and Finland... She could still remain an enormous Power, but far less advantageously posted for aggression on her neighbors"[217] (Bell, 1936: vol. II, p. 105).

Bell recounted how in 1837 a Circassian prince:

"... pointed out the sacred spot (as they justly esteem it) where Daud Bey [David Urquhart] had held (just three years ago in 1834) his meeting with the chieftains of this neighborhood, and first inspired them with the idea of combining themselves with the other inhabitants of the mountain provinces as a nation, under one government and standard" (Bell, vol. I, p. 166).

Urquhart had persuaded another Briton, James Stanislaus Bell, who had chartered the vessel as merchant, to dispatch it contrary to the advice of Ambassador Ponsonby. Bell, ostensibly a merchant but whose interests also extended fat beyond commerce, remained active in the Circassian cause until 1840. He stayed in Circassia for long periods during the years 1837-1839, accompanying the Circassians on raids behind the Russian lines and publishing in 1840 the most comprehensive first-hand account of the Circassian resistance struggle available (Henze, 1990: p. 32).

These unofficial British representatives and activities in Circassia were eager to persuade both the British public and the government that support for Circassian independence would be in the interest of commercial endeavor and British political ideals (Ibid: p. 33).

Additionally, under a secret article the Turks would close the Dardanelles to British and French warships while allowing Russian warships into the Mediterranean. This led to an anti-Russian agitation in England. In 1834, David Urquhart went to Circassia and made contact with the rebels. In 1836, he was captured in the Vixen. From 1837 to 1840 or later James Stanislaus Bell, Edmond Spencer and J. A Longworth of the Times were also in Circassia. All three published memoirs. All four have been accused of implying that they have more influence on the British government than they in fact had and offering the Circassians false hope of British support that would probably not happen.

For example, on arrival in Circassia, Edmund Spencer reported:

"I was shown several copies of the Portfolio containing their declaration of independence, translated into Turkish, one of which every prince and noble

---

217. Palmerston to Russell, 26 May 1854

carries about with him, whether he can read it or not, and regards with the same veneration as the Turks do the Quran. Whenever they sally forth on a warlike excursion, the national banner is carried at the head of the party, and at every general assembly, it is exhibited in some conspicuous place... This circumstance, alone, has given an accession of moral strength, and a confidence in the justness of their cause, with the certainty of ultimately triumphing, that the Russians will find extremely difficult to overcome, and renders the final issue of the contest more than doubtful, even should the mountaineers be left to their own limited resources" (Spencer: vol. II, p. 265).

In November 1836 the Russian military brig, Ajax detained the British schooner Vixen in the seaport Sudzhuk-Kale[218]. At the moment of detention, 8 guns, 28,800 pounds of gunpowder, and a significant amount of other weapons had already been unloaded. This was deemed a provocation by the Russians, instigated by the first secretary of the British embassy in Constantinople David Urquhart. The Polish immigrants also participated in the organization of the incident. The crew received instructions to go in Sudzhuk-Kale where meeting with a Russian cruiser was almost inevitable. The owner of a schooner was recommended not to avoid it, but, on the contrary, to search for this meeting in every possible way (Henze, 2007).

The reaction in London to the seizure was one of outrage. The Conservatives brought up in parliament a question on the legality of Circassia being under the jurisdiction of the Russian empire. Russia was threatened with war. After angry statements from London Nicholas I of Russia ordered the army and fleet into a condition of raised battle readiness. The schooner, according to the instruction, was confiscated, and its crew was sent to Constantinople.

The Russian government was well aware that these British adventurers played a significant role in uniting the Circassians. However, this awareness caused exaggerations about the British involvements in the Caucasus to some extent. In Russia, there was some kind of xenophobia for the external involvements in its affairs. Russia's reactions to the British or Ottoman contacts with the mountaineers of the Caucasus seemed to be a result of this mood. However, the uneasiness of the Russian government about the British involvements did not produce any important crises with the exception of the Vixen affair. According to Luxenburg, Russia was unwilling to turn the issue into an international matter, and to solve its "internal affair" by using its own means and methods (Luxenburg, 1998: pp. 108-109).

The conflict threatened to develop into war between Russia and Britain, but by April 1837, relations had settled down. Urquhart was withdrawn to London.

---

218. nowadays Novorossiysk

Britain was reluctant to antagonize Russia further, as it could not find a continental ally willing to lend support in a war. The official answer of the government and the Liberal Party to an inquiry by the Conservatives stated that Russia owned Circassia lawfully under the Adrianople peace treaty. Russia, therefore, continued its blockade of the east coast of Black sea. The conflict became one of a number of episodes of Russian-British rivalry of the 1830s and 1840s. They were eventually to contribute to the Crimean War.

After invasion of Circassia, Stratford Canning[219] was first one who had raised the Circassian Question for discussion in the House of Lords in June 1864, and Mr. H. Seymour had likewise raised the issue in the House of Commons in the July. It was an issue that attracted British interest closely after three decades of their first involvements in Circassia (Henze, 2007).

Apart from the political concerns over the expansion of the Russian Empire, general public sympathy was also stimulated for the Circassians following numerous updates in the Press about their suffering. In 1862, this was added to by a Circassian delegation visiting the United Kingdom in the hope of gaining British assistance. They visited major cities up and down the country, including London, Manchester, Edinburgh and Dundee, raising awareness of their plight among the British public. This had even led to public lobbying of government for the Circassian cause. Those people of Dundee who had received the Circassian delegation in a public meeting expressed a unanimous vote of sympathy for the people of Circassia (Figure. 12).

---

219. Viscount Stratford de Radcliffe

Maps

(Map. 01) Circassian Tribal Composition 1774-1780
(Source: http://abkhazworld.com/aw/abkhazians/language/648-abkhazo-adyghean-languages-chirikba)

(Map. 02) North Caucasus 1767-1783 by Andrew Andersen
(Source: https://andrewandersenwriter.wordpress.com/2017/03/22/caucasus-russian-atrocities-in-the-north-18th-20th-centuries/)

(Map. 03) Circassia in the new division by Walid Hakuz
(Source: https://tambooosh.files.wordpress.com/2016/12/4e315-occupiedcircassia.jpg?w\u003d820\u0026h\u003d341)

(Map. 04) Topography of North Caucasus by Geopolitical Futures
(Source: https://geopoliticalfutures.com/wp-content/uploads/2017/10/north-caucasus-topography.jpg?utm_source=GPF+-+Paid+Newsletter&utm_campaign=f99b47de48-RSS_EMAIL_CAMPAIGN_Deep_Dive&utm_medium=email&utm_term=0_7 2b76c0285-f99b47de48-240022413)

(Map. 05) Geopolitical situation of North Caucasus by GRID-Arendal
(Source: http://old.grida.no/graphicslib/detail/the-caucasus-ecoregion-topographic-map_a6b6)

(Map. 06) Administrative Division of North Caucasus 1929-1932 by Arthur Tsutsiev
(Source: https://abovyangroup.files.wordpress.com/2015/02/tsutsiev-full-map.jpg)

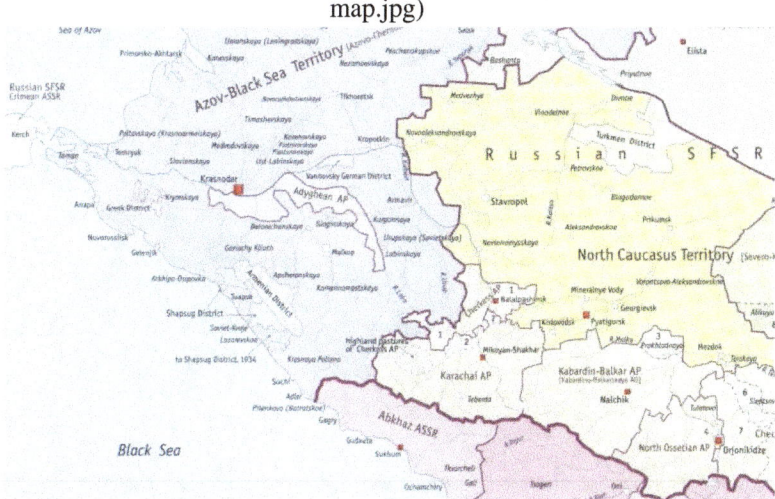

(Map. 07) Linguistic Distribution of Circassians by Christian Bakken
   (Source: https://apps.cndls.georgetown.edu/projects/borders/items/show/283)

(Map. 08) Maykop Culture in Bronze Age
   (Source: https://www.revolvy.com/main/index.php?s=Maykop+culture)

(Map. 09) Sites of Scythians – Sarmatians in North Caucasus
(Source: http://drakenberg.weebly.com/scythians.html)

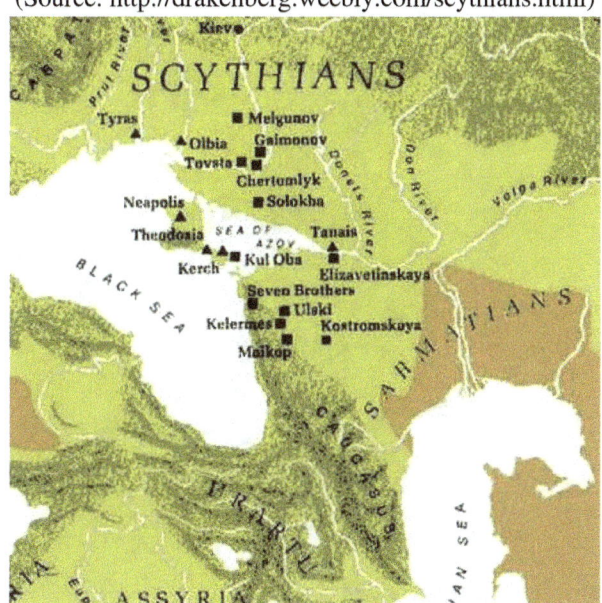

(Map. 10) Hun in North Caucasus
(Source: https://tariganter.wordpress.com/2016/01/23/the-turkish-jewish-khazar/)

(Map. 11) Khazar Khaganate in North Caucasus
(Source: https://www.bibliotecapleyades.net/imagenes_sociopol/khazar03_03.jpg)

(Map. 12) Queen Tamar's realms
(Source: https://artemisiasroyalden.files.wordpress.com/2013/01/672px-geor_tamro1.gif)

(Map. 13) Mongol Invasion of Caucasus in 13th Century
(Source: http://mapwalk2013.clevelandhistory.org/hulegu/)

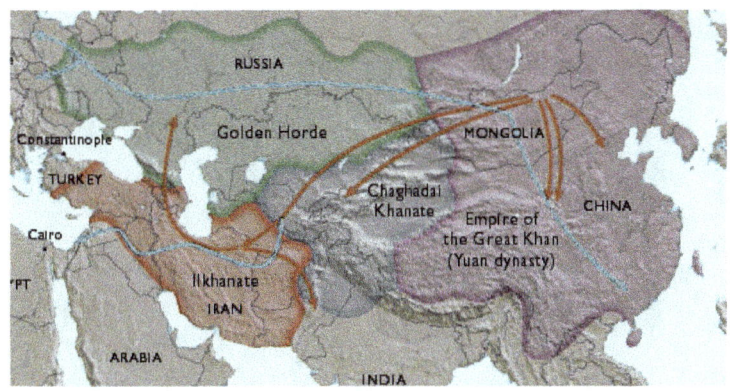

(Map. 14) Mamluk Dynasty
(Source: http://epicworldhistory.blogspot.com/2012/06/mamluk-dynasties-in-egypt.html)

(Map. 15) Russo-Ottoman War 1735–1739
 (Source: https://commons.wikimedia.org/wiki/File:Russo-Turkish_War_of_1735-1739.svg)

(Map. 16) Caucasian War in 19th Century
 (Source: https://www.edmaps.com/html/caucasus.html)

(Map. 17) Caucasian Military Line in 1858
(Source: http://peripheralhistories.blogspot.com/2017/05/russian-little-russian-hardly-russian.html)

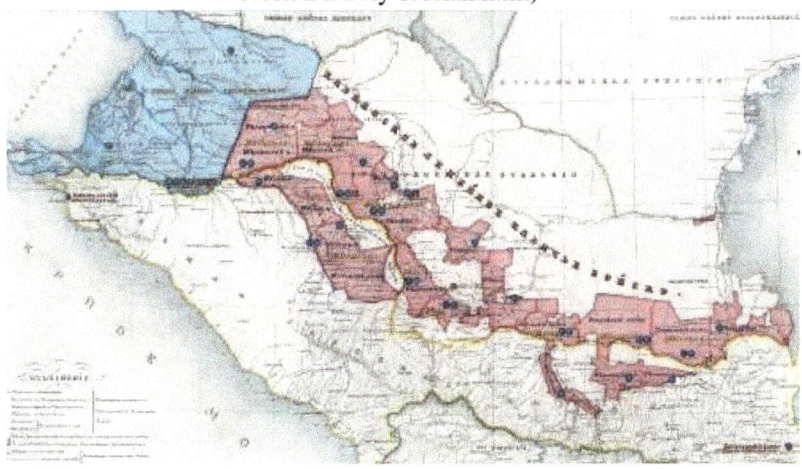

(Map. 18) Russian Expansion in the Caucasus in 1783-1878 by Andrew Andersen
(Source: http://euromaidanpress.com/2017/02/16/the-unsung-lament-russian-atrocities-in-caucasus/)

(Map. 19) Caucasians before Russian Conquest in 19th Century
(Source:
https://www.reddit.com/r/MapPorn/comments/1xn5ny/ethnic_groups_of_the_ca
ucasus_before_the_russian/)

(Map. 20) Circassia in 1840 by James Bell
(Source: http://www.bivouac.ru/2016/07/chernomorskoye-poberegie-
kavkaza.html)

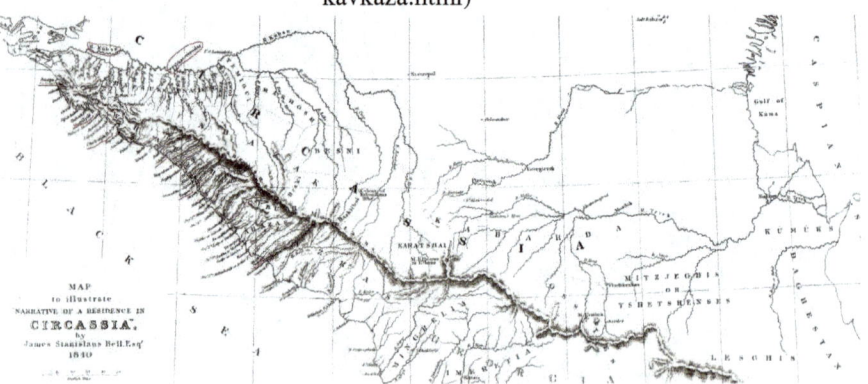

(Map. 21) Circassian Exile to Ottoman Empire
(Source: http://www.wikiwand.com/en/Circassia)

(Map. 22) Turkic Kingdoms around Caspian Sea in 15-16th Centuries
(Source:
http://www.historyfiles.co.uk/images/FarEast/CentralAsia/Map_CentralAsia_AD1500_max.jpg)

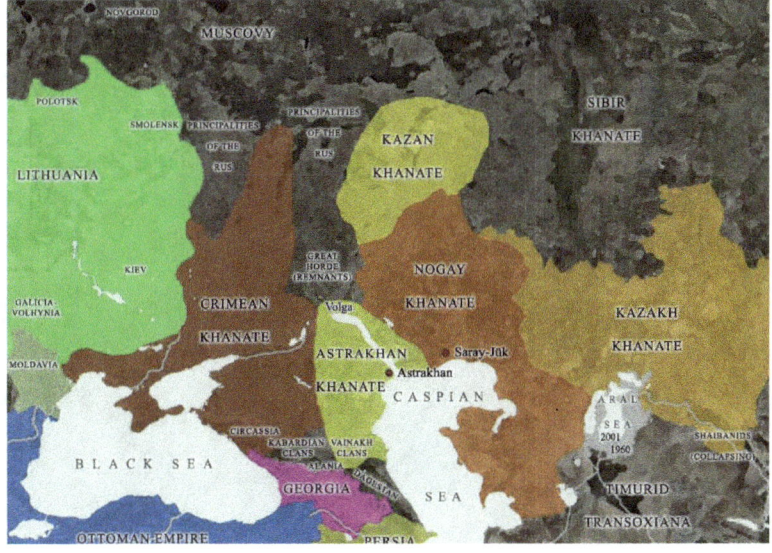

(Map. 23) Russo – Persian Wars's results Map in the Caucasus
  (Source: http://www.iranreview.org/file/cms/files/782px-Gulistan-Treaty.jpg)

(Map. 24) Circassian Dispersion in Middle East by NCRP
  (Source: https://joshuaproject.net/assets/media/profiles/maps/m11675.png)

(Map. 25) Caucasus in 1917-1919

(Source: https://www.euratlas.net/history/hisatlas/ussr/191917CC.jpg)

(Map. 26) Mountain Republic by stampworldhistory

(Source: http://www.stampworldhistory.com/wp-content/uploads/2015/03/Mountain-republic.png)

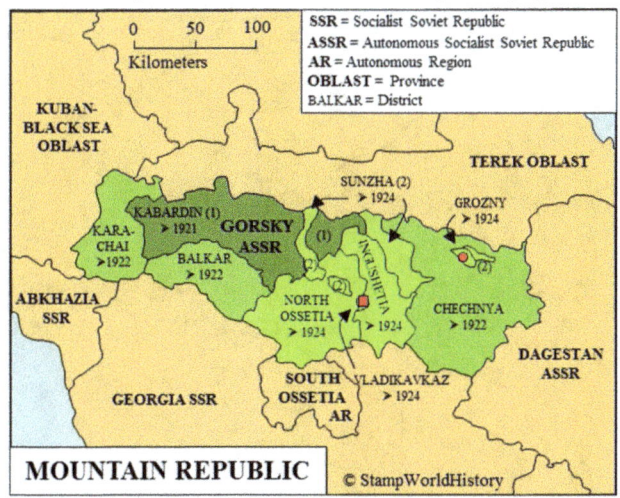

(Map. 27) Abkhaz-Adygheans in Turkey
(Source:
https://upload.wikimedia.org/wikipedia/commons/thumb/d/df/CircassianinTu.png/300px-CircassianinTu.png)

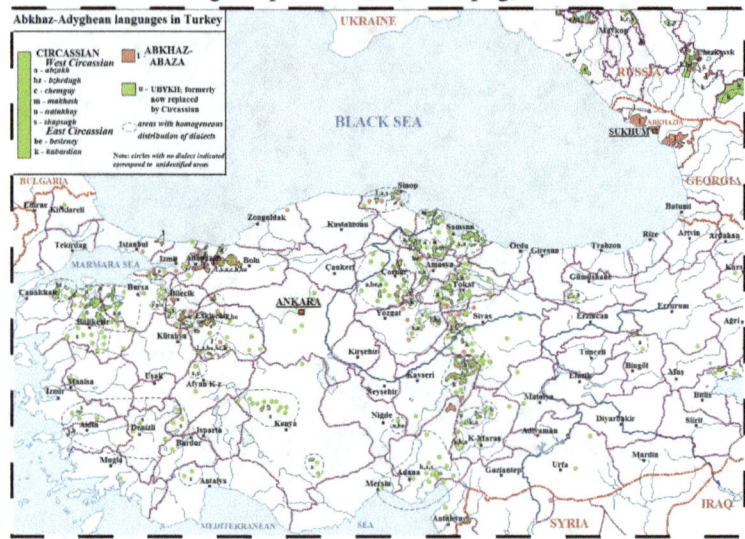

(Map. 28) North Caucasus administrative in 1920's
(Source: http://www.wikiwand.com/ru/)

Figures

(Figure. 01) Flag of Circassia
(Source: https://upload.wikimedia.org/wikipedia/commons/1/16/Flag_of_Adygea.svg)

(Figure. 02) Circassian Traditional Clothing by Andynapso
(Source: https://upload.wikimedia.org/wikipedia/commons/d/d5/CircassianPhoto.jpg)

(Figure. 03) Mount Elbrus by Maks Alpert
(Source: https://tr.sputniknews.com/foto/201507231016712553/)

(Figure. 04) Circassian Music instruments
(Source: http://toroyloco.blogspot.com/2010/07/adyghe.html)

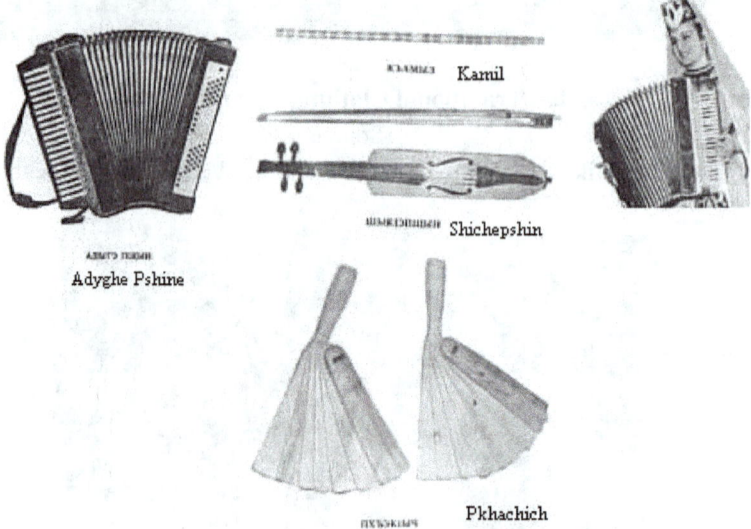

(Figure. 05) Circassian Dance
(Source: http://e-onomastics.blogspot.com/2013/03/international-conference-problems-of.html)

(Figure. 06) Silver reindeer figurine the Koban Culture
(Source: https://pl.pinterest.com/pin/314407617708166964/)

(Figure. 07) Golden ox figurine found in the Maykop kurgan in Hermitage Museum
(Source: https://www.pinterest.com/pin/20336635790535848/)

(Figure. 08) Tamar the Great Fresco at the church of Dormition in Vardzia
(Source:
https://i.pinimg.com/originals/d4/0e/7a/d40e7a9ff15963eb77f1f52cd507f2ad.jpg
)

(Figure. 09) Picture of Crimean War - Episode of Sebastopol Siege
  (Source: http://historylearning.com/the-crimean-war-1853-1856/)

(Figure. 10) Picture of Murid War - Episode of Akhatle Battle in 1841
  (Source: http://oshten.blogspot.com/2012/01/21-1763-1864.html)

(Figure. 11) Picture of Sefer Bey Zanuko in 1845
(Source:
https://upload.wikimedia.org/wikipedia/commons/d/db/Circassian_prince.jpg)

(Figure. 12) Picture of Circassian Envoys to England - Hadji Hassan Effendi (Left) Constan Okhoo Ismael Effendi (Right) in 1862
(Source: https://www.alamy.com/stock-photo/effendi.html)

(Figure. 12) Photo of Prince Adam Czartoryski by Felix Nadar in 1861
(Source: https://superhistoria.pl/xix-wiek/34269/Ksiaze-Adam-Jerzy-Czartoryski-rosyjski-minister-i-polski-patriota.html)

(Figure. 13) Picture of Michał Czajkowski
(Source: https://upload.wikimedia.org/wikipedia/commons/4/41/Micha%C5%82_Czajkowski_%281804-1886%29.jpg)

(Figure. 14) Picture of Count Mikhail Tarielovich Loris-Melikov I
(Source: https://www.runivers.ru/images/date/2010_february/24/s.jpg)

(Figure. 15) Flag - Mountainous Republic of the Northern Caucasus
(Source: https://vignette.wikia.nocookie.net/future/images/6/6e/NorthernCaucasus.png/revision/latest/scale-to-width-down/2000?cb=20180502024950)

(Figure. 16) Picture of General Anton Denikin
(Source: https://russiapedia.rt.com/files/prominent-russians/military/anton-denikin/anton-denikin_5-t.jpg)

(Figure. 17) Picture of Russian propaganda in Circassia - 450 years together

(Source: my field studies)

(Figure. 18) Flag – Confederation of Mountain People of Caucasus
(Source:
https://ipfs.io/ipfs/QmXoypizjW3WknFiJnKLwHCnL72vedxjQkDDP1mXWo6
uco/I/m/KHNK.png)

(Figure. 19) Picture of Yusup Soslambekov
(Source:
https://www.google.com/url?sa=i&rct=j&q=&esrc=s&source=images&cd=&ca
d=rja&uact=8&ved=2ahUKEwjnjp_2kJLdAhVml4sKHewKDh0QjRx6BAgBE
AU&url=https%3A%2F%2Fwww.gettyimages.com%2Fvideos%2Fchechnya%3
Fpage%3D2&psig=AOvVaw14Jlrp2OKQUAm-
z5_holr6&ust=1535627561970980)

Bibliography

Abtorkhanov, Abdurahman & Bennigsen Broxup, Marie (1992). *The North Caucasus Barrier: The Russian Advance towards the Muslim World*. London: C. Hurst & Co LTD. (Online access: https://www.thefreelibrary.com/The+North+Caucasus+Barrier%3A+The+Russian+Advance+Towards+the+Muslim...-a013834712)

Acton, John Emerich Edward Dalberg (1907). *The Cambridge Modern History*. New York, The Macmillan Company. Vo. VI. (Online access: https://archive.org/details/cambridgemodern15benigoog)

Adighe, R. (1956). *'Cherkess Cultural Life'*. Caucasian Review, Munich (CRM): Vol. 2.

Adygea NatPress (2010). *В Иордании началась трансляция фильмов об Адыгее*. [In Jordan, began airing movies on Adygea] (in Russian). Retrieved 6 May 2010.

Aksoy, Zeynep (2003). *Çerkes Teavün Cemiyeti*. (in Turkish) Toplumsal Tarih: 117.

Albin, Pierre (1912). *Les grands traités politiques*. Recueil des principaux textes diplomatique depuis 1815 jusqu'à nos jours. Acte général du congrès de paris. Paris: F.Alcan.

Aliev, U. (1927). *Karachai*. Rostov-on-Don: Krainatsizdat.

Allen, W. E. D. & Muratoff, Paul (1953). *Caucasian Battlefields: A History of the Wars on the Turco-Caucasian Border 1828-1921*. Cambridge.

Anchalabze, George (2009). *The Vainakhs; the Chechen and Ingush*. Editor: N. Gelashvili, Translated into English by T. Paichadze. Tbilisi: Caucasian House – CircassianWorld. (Online access: https://www.circassianworld.com/pdf/The_Vainakhs_George_Anchabadze.pdf)

Arbuthnot, N. (1988). *A Re-evaluation of the Proposed Connection between the Nart Sagas and the Arthurian Legends*. MA Thesis in Cultural Anthropology, McMaster University, Toronto, British Columbia, Canada.

Atalikov, V. (2010). *'The Caucasus: European diaries from the 13th–18th centuries'*. Issue 3.

Ataman, M. (2002). *'Leadership Change: Ozal Leadership and Restructuring in Turkish Foreign Policy'*. Alternatives: Vol.1, No.1, spring.

Avagyan, Arsen (2004). *Osmanlı İmparatorluğu ve Kemalist Türkiye'nin Devlet-İktidar Sisteminde Çerkesler*. Istanbul: Belge Yayınları.

Avezac, M. (de) (1839). *'Recueil de voyages et de mémoires publié par la Société de Géographie'*. No.4, Paris.

Axel, Brian (2004). *'Context of Diaspora. Cultural Anthropology'*. 19(1). (Online access: http://www.urbanlab.org/articles/Axel%20Context%20of%20diaspora.pdf)

Aydemir, İzzet (1991). *Muhaceretteki Çerkes Aydınları*. Ankara.

Aydin,M. (2000). *'Turkish Policy toward the Caucasus'*. The Quarterly Journal: No.3, September.

Azrael, Jeremy R., and Emil A. Payin (1998). *Conflict and Consensus in Ethno-Political and Center-Peripheral Relations in Russia*. Rand Institute, Moocow. (Online access: https://www.rand.org/pubs/conf_proceedings/CF139.html)

Babich, L. (2003). '*Klanovaya struktura obshchestva i yeye vliyaniye na sovremennuyu politicheskuyu situatsiyu*'. Tsentral'naya Aziya i Kavkaz, 25, 1. (Online Access: www.ca-c.org/online/2003/journalJus/cac-01l00.contrus.shtml)

Baddeley, John F. (1908). *Russian Conquest of the Caucasus*. Chapter V.

Barry, E. (2011). *Georgia Says Russia Committed Genocide in 19th Century*. The New York Times. May 20. (Online Access: https://www.nytimes.com/2011/05/21/world/europe/21georgia.html?emc=eta1)

Bauer, L. (2007). *The Linguistics Student's Handbook*. Edinburgh.

Baytugan, Barsabi (1971). *The North Caucasus Studies on the Soviet Union*. Vo. XI.

BBC News (2009). '*Russia ends Chechnya operation*'. 14 April. (Online Access: http://news.bbc.co.uk/2/hi/europe/8001495.stm)

Bell, C.F. & Lord Palmerston (1936). *Palmerston to Russell*, 26 May 1854, as cited in Herbert. London: Longmans Green, vol. II.

Bell, J. S. (2007). '*Journal of a residence in Circassia during the year's 1837, 1838 and 1839*', Nalchik, Russia, El-Fa. (Online access: https://archive.org/details/journalofresiden01belluoft)

Berzegov, Aliy (2008). '*Teofil Lapinski: Hero and Leader of the Circassian War for Independence*'. (Part One) Publication: North Caucasus Weekly Volume: 9 Issue: 22. (Online Access: https://jamestown.org/program/teofil-lapinski-hero-and-leader-of-the-circassian-war-for-independence-part-one/)

Besleney, Z. A. (2014). *Circassian Diaspora in Turkey*. A Political History. London: Routledge.

Bezanis, Lowell (1994). '*Soviet Muslim Emigrés in the Republic of Turkey*'. Central Asian Survey, 13(1). (Online access: https://www.tandfonline.com/doi/abs/10.1080/02634939408400852)

Biersteker, Thomas J. and Cynthia Weber, eds. (1996). *State Sovereignty as Social Construct*. Cambridge: Cambridge University Press. (Online access: https://trove.nla.gov.au/work/21678015)

Blank, S. and Kim, Y. (2016). '*The North Caucasus: Russia's Other War*'. Journal of Slavic Military Studies, Vol. 29, No. 2.

Bobrovnikov, V. (2001). '*Al-Azhar and shari'a courts in the twentieth century Caucasus*'. Middle Eastern Studies, 37:4.

Bram, Ch. (1999). *Circassian re-immigration to the Caucasus - Routes and Roots: Emigration in a global perspective*. Ed. by S. Weil, Magnes, Jerusalem.

Brandell, Inga and Marie Carlson and Önver Cetrez (Ed.) (2015). '*Borders and the Changing Boundaries of Knowledge*'. Talking about the silence and the break by Setenay Nil Dogan.

Swedish Research Institute in Istanbul. vol. 22. (Online access: http://www.srii.org/content/upload/documents/e7aaeef6-2f8c-4c81-b4da-fbef770d50dd.pdf)

Brenton, T. (2018). *'Russia and The West: On the Brink'*. lobelog: 2 June. (Online access: https://lobelog.com/russia-and-the-west-on-the-brink/)

Brock, P. (1956). *'The Fall of Circassia: A Study in Private Diplomacy'*. The English Historical Review, Vo.71, No. 280. (Online access: http://www.21mayis.org/content/pdf/war/1956_The_Fall_of_Circassia.pdf)

Broxup, M. B. (ed.) (1992). *The North Caucasus Barrier: The Russian Advance towards the Muslim World*. St Martin's Press: New York.

Bubenok, O. (2015). *'The Adyghe Factor in The Ethnopolitical Development of The Northern Caucasus'*. Central Asia and The Caucasus: Volume 16, Issue 2.

Bullough, O. (2012). *'Sochi 2014 Winter Olympics: The Circassians Cry Genocide'*. Newsweek, May 21. (Online Access: www.newsweek.com/sochi-2014-winter-olympics-circassians-cry-genocide-64893)

Burney, Ch. (2004). *Historical dictionary of the Hittites. Historical Dictionaries of Ancient Civilizations and Historical Era*. Lanham, MD: Scarecrow Press.

Bushuev, S. (1959). *Istoriia Severo-Osetinskoi ASSR*. Moscow: Izdatel'stvo Akademii Nauk SSSR.

Caucasian Knot (2012). *Темой Дня репатрианта в Адыгее, Кабардино-Балкарии и Грузии стали проблемы черкесской общины Сирии*. [The topic for Repatriant's Day in Agydea, Kabardio-Balkaria and Georgia was the problems of the Circassian community in Syria]. (Online access: http://www.kavkaz-uzel.eu/articles/210595/)

Caucasian Knot (2015). *'Friends of assassinated Aslan Zhukov hold protest action in Karachai-Circassia'*. (Online access: http://www.eng.kavkaz-uzel.eu/articles/12827/)

Çelikpala, M. (2006). *'From Immigrants to Diaspora: Influence of the North Caucasian Diaspora in Turkey'*. Middle Eastern Studies: Vol. 42, No. 3 (May). Taylor & Francis, Ltd. (Online Access: https://www.jstor.org/stable/4284462)

Census (2013). *The official results of the 2010 All-Russia Population Census*. (Online access: http://demoscope.ru/weekly/ssp/rus_nac_10.php)

Cherkasov, A. and Vladimir G. Ivantsov, Michal Smigel, Violetta S. Molchanova (2015). *'The Daily Life and Morals of Circassian Society: A Historical-Comparative Investigation based on sources from the period between the Mid-16th and the First Half of the 19th centuries'*. Brukenthal: Acta Musei, X.01. (Online access: http://incfar.net/images/our_stats/pdf/brukenthalacta-musei-x1istorie.pdf)

Chirikba, V. A. (2006). *'Abkhaz Community Abroad'*. Apsny press. (Online access: http://www.apsny.ru/community/community.php?page=content/community_a/community_a.htm)

Chisholm, Hugh (1911). *'Circassia. Encyclopedia Britannica'*. vol. 6 (11th Ed.). Cambridge University Press. (Online access: https://www.studylight.org/encyclopedias/bri/c/circassia.html)

Civil Georgia (2015). *'At Geneva talks Russia Says Georgia's NATO Integration Poses Security Threat to the Region'*. Civil.ge: 15 December. (Online Access: http://civil.ge/eng/article.php?id=28403)

Colarusso, John (1991). *'Circassian Repatriation: When Culture is Stronger than Politics'*. The World & I, November issue. Washington, D.C.: The Washington Times Publishing Corporation.

Colarusso, John (1994). *'Circassians'*. Encyclopedia of World Cultures, David Levinson (ed.), vol. 6, Inner Eurasia and China , Paul Friedrich and Norma Diamond (eds.), Boston, Massachusetts: G. K. Hall & Co. (Online access: http://www.encyclopedia.com/places/commonwealth-independent-states-and-baltic-nations/cis-and-baltic-political-geography-110)

Comins-Richmond, W. (2004). *'Legal Pluralism in the Northwest Caucasus: The Role of Sharia Courts'*. Religion, State & Society. Vol. 32, No.1.

Crisis Group (2012). *The North Caucasus: The Challenges of Integration (i), Ethnicity and Conflict*. Europe Report N°220.

Curtis, William Eleroy (2008). *Around the Black Sea. Asia Minor, Armenia, Caucasus, Circassia, Dagestan, the Crimea, Romania*. New York, 1911 - reprinted: LULU PR. (Online access: https://books.google.pl/books/about/Around_the_Black_Sea_Asia_Minor_Armenia.html?id=tt-_jwEACAAJ&redir_esc=y)

Dankoff, R. (2004). *An Ottoman Mentality: The World of Evliya Çelebi*. BRILL.

Deng, Francis M. (1995). *War of Visions: Conflict of Identities in the Sudan*. Washington, DC: Brookings.

Derluguian, Georgi M. (2009). *A World History of Noxchi*. Yale University.

Doğan, S. N. (2009). *Formations of Diaspora Nationalism: The Case of Circassians in Turkey*. PhD diss., Sabancı University, Istanbul.

Dostál, P., (1999). *'Ethnicity, mobilization and territory: an overview of recent experiences'*. In: Act Universitatis Carolinae. Geographica, No.1.

Dowling, Timothy C. (2014). *'Russia at War: From the Mongol Conquest to Afghanistan, Chechnya, and Beyond'*. Vo. 02, ABC-CLIO.

Dowling, Timothy C., ed. (2014). *Russia at War*. Santa Barbara, California: ABC-CLIO.

Dubrovin, N. (1886). *'History of Russian wars and rule in the Caucasus'*. Vo.11, St. Petersburg.

Džahazaeva, I.A. (2011). Processy administrativno-teritorialnogo razmeževanija v Karačaje v 1920–130 gg, *"Naučno-teoretičeskij Žurnal, Naučne Problemy Gumanitarnych Issledovanij"*. issue 6.

Dzutsati, V. (2015). *'International Circassian Association's Closeness to Moscow Backfires'*. Publication: Eurasia Daily Monitor Volume: 12 Issue: 127.

Dzutsati, V. (2016). *'Strategic Assessment: Russian Policy in the North Caucasus Remains in Flux'*. Eurasia Daily Monitor Volume: 13 Issue: 175. (Online Access: https://jamestown.org/program/russian-policy-north-caucasus-remains-flux/)

Dzutsati, Valery (2010). *'Murder of Circassian Activist Unsettles Multi-Ethnic Karachaevo-Cherkessia'*. The Jamestown Foundation. Eurasia Daily Monitor Volume: 7 Issue: 52. (Online access: https://jamestown.org/program/murder-of-circassian-activist-unsettles-multi-ethnic-karachaevo-cherkessia-2/).

Economist (2012). *Home thoughts from abroad: Circassians mourn the past—and organize for the future*. (Online access: http://www.economist.com/node/21555892?fsrc=scn/tw/te/ar/homethoughtsfromabroad)

Elot.ru (2010). (Online Access: http://elot.ru/index.php?option=com_content&task=view&id=2075&itemid=1)

Elot.ru (2011). *The creation of the Council of Circassian organizations* – the first step towards a unified organization in Russia' (in Russian). (Online Access: http://www.elot.ru/index.php?option=com_content&task=view&id=2213&Itemid=1)

Emerson, M. (2008). *'Post-Mortem on Europe's First War of the 21st Century'*. Centre for European Policy Studies: August. (Online Access: http://aei.pitt.edu/9382/2/9382.pdf)

Enteen, G. M. (2002). *'Recent Writings about Soviet Historiography'*. Slavic Review 61 (2).

Epifantsev, Andrey (2009). *Кавказская война: геноцид, которого не было*. [The Caucasian War. The Genocide that wasn't], Agentstvo politich-eskih novostey. (Online access: https://www.apn.ru/publications/article22023.htm)

Erciyes, J. C. (2014). *'Diaspora of Diaspora: Adyge-Abkhaz Returnees in the Ancestral Homeland'*. Diaspora: a journal of transnational studies. Summer.

Erikson, E.H. (1964). *Insight and responsibility*. New York: Norton. (Online access: http://journals.sfu.ca/rpfs/index.php/rpfs/article/view/80/79)

Esadze, Semen (1993). *Pokorenie zapadnogo Kavkaza i okonchanie Kavkazskoi voiny*. Maykop.

Faḍlullāh Hamadānī, Rashīd al-Dīn. (2016) *Jame o Tavarikh* (Tarikh Mobarak e Qazani), [فضل الله همطئی، رشیدالدین. (1394) جامع التواریخ (تاریخ مبارک غازانی) مصحح: محمد روشن، مصطفی موسوی،یاشر: مرکز پژوهشی میراث مکتوب،یهران.] Mosaheh: Mohammad Roshan, Mostafa Musavi, Nasher: Markaze Pashouheshi Miras e Maktou, Tehran.

Falkowski, M. (2015). *'Ramzanistan: Russia's Chechen Problem'*. Warsaw: Centre for Eastern Studies, Point of View, No. 54.

Fearon, J. (1999). *What is Identity (As we now use the word)?* (Unpublished manuscript). Stanford University, California.

Feltshinsky, Y. and Litvinenko, A. (2007). *Blowing Up Russia*. Terror from Within, Gibson Square Books, London.

Ferris-Rotman, Amie (2011). *Clashes in Russia's Caucasus kill 10 rebels*. (Online access: https://ca.reuters.com/article/topNews/idCATRE73S5IQ20110429)

Fischer, S. (2016). The Conflict over Abkhazia and South Ossetia in Light of the Crisis over Ukraine..

Fischer, S. (ed.) (2016). *Not Frozen: the Unresolved Conflicts over Transnistria, Abkhazia, South Ossetia and Nagorno-Karabakh in Light of the Crisis in Ukraine*. SWP, Research Paper 9, Berlin: German Institute for International and Security Affairs.

Gadlo, A.V. (1994). *Etnicheskaia istoriaSevernogo Kavkaza X-XIII vv.* St. Petersburg.

Gafarli, Orkhan (2014). *'The role of north Caucasus diaspora groups in Turkey-Russia relations'*. Turkish policy quarterly: VOLUME 13 NUMBER 1. (Online access: http://www.bilgesam.org/Images/Dokumanlar/0-30-2014061125vol_13-no_1-gafarli.pdf)

Gammer, M. (1995). *Unity, Diversity and Conflict in the Northern Caucasus*. In Yaacov Ro'i, ed., Muslim Eurasia: Conflicting Legacies. London: Frank Cass.

Gammer, M. (2014). *'Separatism in the Northern Caucasus'*. Caucasus Survey, 1:2.

Gammer, Moshe (2004). *'The Caspian Region'*. Volume 1: A Re-Emerging Region, London: Routledge. (Online access: https://www.google.com/books?hl=en&lr=&id=KPKQAgAAQBAJ&oi=fnd&pg=PP1&dq =Gammer,+The+Caspian+Region:+a+Re-emerging+Region,+London:+Routledge&ots=SrRkb2V7dp&sig=Gmr1ztWjoErfky4TDhbj SCtKucM)

Gammer, Moshe (2006). *'Ethno-Nationalism, Islam and the State in the Caucasus: Post-Soviet Disorder'*. Central Asian Studies, 1st Edition. Routledge.

Gardanov V. K. (1967). *Social System of Adyghe People*.

Gardanov, V. (1967). *Ekonomicheskoe razvitie Kabardy i Balkarii v XVIII v*. In Istoriia Kabardino-Balkarskoi ASSR Tom I, edited by T.Kh. Kalmykov. Moscow: Nauka.

Gellner, E. (2002). *Nacionalismus. Brno: Centrum pro studium demokracie a kultury*.

Gingeras, Ryan (2011). *'Sorrowful Shores: Violence, Ethnicity, and the End of the Ottoman Empire 1912-1923'*. Oxford Studies in Modern European History, 1st Edition.

Gleason, John Howes (1950). *The Genesis of Russophobia in Great Britain*. Massachusetts.

Glen E. Howard (2012). Volatile Borderland: Russia and the North Caucasus. Washington, DC: Jamestown Foundation.

Glenny, Misha (2012). *The Balkans: Nationalism, War, and the Great Powers, 1804-2011*. Penguin Publishing Group.

Gobejishvili, Nikoloz (2014). *Interrelation of Colchian and Koban Cultures According to Burial Constructions and Funerary Customs*. Late Bronze – Early Iron Age. (Online access: http://www.spekali.tsu.ge/pdf/8_80_en.pdf)

Goble, P. (2017). *'Inter-Ethnic Land Conflicts Threaten Borders in the North Caucasus'*. Eurasia Daily Monitor, Vol. 14, Issue 98, The Jamestown Foundation. (Online Access:

https://jamestown.org/program/inter-ethnic-land-conflicts-threaten-borders-in-north-caucasus/)

Goble, Paul (2009). 'Circassian Youth Seek Radical Renewal of National Movement'. Window on Eurasia. (Online Access: http://windowoneurasia.blogspot.com/2009/09/window-on-eurasia-circassian-youth-seek.html)

Gökçe, Cemal (1979). '*Kafkasya ve Osmanlı İmparatorluğu'nun Kafkasya Siyaseti*'. Istanbul: Şamil Vakfı.

Guibernau, Montserrat and John Rex (1997). *The Ethnicity Reader: Nationalism, Multiculturalism and Migration*. Cambridge, UK: Polity Press; Malden, MA: Blackwell Publishers,

Haindrava, I. (2011). '*Georgia's recognition of the Circassian genocide in the context of Georgian-Abkhaz-Russian relations*'. 13 Jul. (Online Access: https://www.international-alert.org/blog/georgia%E2%80%99s-recognition-circassian-genocide-context-georgian-abkhaz-russian-relations)

Hajda, L. and Beissinger, M., eds. (1990). *The Nationalities Factor in Soviet Politics and Society*. Boulder, Co.: Westview.

Halbach, Uwe (2014). *The Circassian Question Russian Colonial History in the Caucasus and a Case of "Long-distance Nationalism"*. SWP Comments 37. (Online access: https://www.swp-berlin.org/fileadmin/contents/products/comments/2014C37_hlb.pdf)

Hammer-Purgstall, Joseph (1856). *Geschichte der Chane der Krim*. Vienna.

Hansen, L. F. (2012). '*Renewed Circassian Mobilization in the North Caucasus 20-years after the Fall of the Soviet Union*'. Journal on Ethnopolitics and Minority Issues in Europe Vol 11, No 2.

Hansen, L. F. (2014). *The Circassian Revival: A Quest for Recognition, Mediated Transnational Mobilisation and Memorialization among a Geographically Dispersed People from the Caucasus*. PhD diss., University of Copenhagen.

Hansen, Lars Funch (2012). '*Renewed Circassian Mobilization in the North Caucasus: Twenty Years After the Fall of the Soviet Union*'. Journal on Ethnopolitics and Minority Issues in Europe 11, no. 2. (Online access: http://www.ecmi.de/fileadmin/downloads/publications/JEMIE/2012/Vol_2_Dezember_2012/6._JEMIE_Hansen.pdf)

Harding, L. (2008). '*Georgia calls on EU for independent inquiry into war*'. The Guardian: 19 November. (Online Access: https://www.theguardian.com/world/2008/nov/19/georgia-russia-eu-media-inquiry)

Hedenskog, J. and Persson, G., Carolina VendilPallin (2016). *Russian Security Policy*.

Henze, Paul B. (1992). *Circassian Resistance to Russia*. London: HURST & CO. (Online access: http://www.circassianworld.com/Circassian_Resistance.pdf)

Henze, Paul B. (1995). *Islam in The North Caucasus, The Example of Chechnia*. Rand Corporation, University of Virginia, (Online access: https://circassianworld.com/pdf/Henze_Islam_NorthCaucasus.pdf)

Hirsch, F. (2005). *Empire of Nations: Ethnographic Knowledge and the Making of the Soviet Union*. Cornell University Press: Ithaca, N.Y.

Hitchens, Keith (2012). *Great Powers, Small Powers: Wallachia and Georgia Confront the Eastern Question, 1768–1802*. In Ivan Biliarsky; Ovidiu Cristea; Anca Oroveanu. The Balkans and Caucasus: Parallel Processes on the Opposite Sides of the Black Sea. Cambridge Scholars Publishing.

Hoiberg, D. H. (ed.) (2010). *Abkhazo-Adyghian languages*. Encyclopedia Britannica. I: A-ak Bayes (15th ed.). Chicago, IL: Encyclopedia Britannica Inc.

Hopkirk, Peter (2001). *'The great game: On Secret Service in High Asia'*. Chapter 12; The Greatest Fortress in the World. Oxford University Press.

Horowitz, Donald L. (1985). *Ethnic Groups in Conflict*. Berkeley, CA: University of California Press.

Hotko S.H. (2005). *'Stary'e cherkesskie sady'. Landshaft i agrikul'tura Severo-Zapadnogo Kavkaza v osveshhenii russkix istochnikov'*. 1864-1914 [The old Circassian gardens. The landscape of agriculture and the Northwest Caucasus in the Russian light sources. 1864-1914]. Moscow, Olma-Press Publ, vol. 1.

Hunter, S. (2006). *'Borders, conflict, and security in the Caucasus: the legacy of the past'*. SAIS Review of International Affairs, vol. 26, no. 1.

Hunter, S. T. (2004). *Islam in Russia: The Politics of Identity and Security*. M. E. Sharpe: Armonk, N.Y.

Hupchick, Dennis P. (2002). *The Balkans: From Constantinople to Communism*. Palgrave Macmillan.

Hurewitz, J.C. (1975). *'The middle east and north Africa in world politics: a documentary record'*. vol.1, European expansion, 1533-1914, new haven. documents No.32.

Ilgener, Ahmet (2013). *Turkey and the North Caucasus: an analysis of internal and domestic relations*. Naval postgraduate school Monterey, California. (Online access: https://www.circassianworld.com/pdf/13Dec_Ilgener_Ahmet.pdf)

Ilgener, Ahmet (2013). *Turkey and the north Caucasus: an analysis of internal and domestic relations*. Monterey, California: Naval Postgraduate School - December.

Inal-Ipa, A. (2012). *The Circassian question and Abkhazia: historical factors and contemporary challenges*. (Online Access: http://abkhazworld.com/aw/analysis/773-the-circassian-question-and-abkhazia-by-arda-inal-ipa)

Interiano, G. (1974). *The daily life and country of the Zikhs, called Circassians Nalchik*.

International Crisis Group (2011). *Georgia-Russia: Learn to Live Like Neighbors*. Europe Briefing N°65 - 8 August. (Online access: https://www.crisisgroup.org/file/1502/download?token=F8Qw7VV7)

International crisis group (2012). *The north Caucasus: the challenges of integration (i), ethnicity and conflict.* Europe Report N°220 – 19 October. (Online access: https://www.ecoi.net/en/file/local/1348833/1226_1350913897_220-the-north-caucasus-the-challenges-of-integration-i-ethnicity-and-conflict.pdf)

International Crisis Group (2012). *Troubled North Caucasus: The Challenges of Integration – Europe.* Report N°220 | 19 October. (Online access: https://www.crisisgroup.org/europe-central-asia/caucasus/north-caucasus/north-caucasus-challenges-integration-i-ethnicity-and-conflict)

Isichei, Elizabeth (1997). *A History of African Societies to 1870.* Cambridge University Press.

ITAR-TASS (1994). *Address to the peoples of the Caucasus by the Russian President Boris N. Yeltsin on the 130th anniversary of the end of the Caucasian War*, Moscow, 18 May.

Ivanova, Mariya (2007). '*The Chronology of the "Maykop Culture" in the North Caucasus: Changing Perspectives*'. Armenian Journal of Near Eastern Studies. II.

Jackson, Kathleen R., and Marat Fidarov (2009). *Essays on the History of the North Caucasus.* HHN Media, New York.

Jaimoukha, A. (1998). *An Introductory Account of Circassian Literature.* Jaimoukha Synthasite (Online access: http://jaimoukha.synthasite.com/circassian-literature.php)

Jaimoukha, Amjad (1998). *An Introductory Account of Circassian Literature.* Jaimoukha Synthasite (Online access: http://jaimoukha.synthasite.com/circassian-literature.php)

Jaimoukha, Amjad (2001). *The Circassian; a handbook.* Curzon; Caucasus World.

Jaimoukha, Amjad (2004). *The Chechens; A Handbook.* Taylor & Francis. (Online access: https://books.google.pl/books/about/The_Chechens.html?id=O56A3HB4jo4C&redir_esc=y)

Jaimoukha, Amjad (2009). *A Descriptive Account, Circassian Religion and Beliefs.* Jaimoukha Synthasite (online access: http://jaimoukha.synthasite.com/circassian-religion.php)

Jaimoukha, Amjad (2009). *Circassian Customs & Traditions.* First published, The International Centre for Circassian Studies. (Online access: https://www.academia.edu/5726392/Circassian_Customs_and_Traditions)

Jaimoukha, Amjad (2010). *Circassian Dance.* Circassian World. (Online access: http://www.circassianworld.com/pdf/Circassian_Dance.pdf)

Javakhishvili, N. (2012). *Coverage of The tragedy public Thought* (later half of the 19th century). Tbilisi State University, 20 December. (Online Access: http://justicefornorthcaucasus.info/?p=1251662239)

Jelen, Libor (2014). *Spatial analysis of ethnopolitical mobilisation in the Caucasus in the 1980s and 1990s.* Bulletin of Geography. Socio–economic Series No. 25. (Online access: http://www.bulletinofgeography.umk.pl/25_2014/Jelen.pdf)

Jersild, A. (2003). *Orientalism and Empire: North Caucasus Mountain Peoples and the Georgian Frontier, 1845–1917.* McGill-Queen's University Press: Montreal.

Jesse, Captain (1841). *Notes of a half-pay in search of health: or, Russia, Circassia, and the Crimea in 1849–40*. London: James Madden and Co.

Kaas, Kaarel (2009). *The Russian Bear on the Warpath against Georgia*. International Centre for Defense Studies. (Online Access: https://icds.ee/the-russian-bear-on-the-warpath-against-georgia/)

Kabardia (1911). Encyclopedia Britannica, vol. 15. (Online access: http://encyclopedia.jrank.org/JUN_KHA/KABARDIA.html)

Kahn, J. (2002). *Federalism, Democratization, and the Rule of Law in Russia*. Oxford University Press: Oxford.

Kale, Ba̧sak (2014). *'Transforming an Empire: The Ottoman Empire's Immigration and Settlement Policies in the Nineteenth and Early Twentieth Centuries'*. Middle Eastern Studies, Vol. 50, No. 2. (Online accesses: http://dx.doi.org/10.1080/00263206.2013.870894)

Kappeler, Andreas (2001). *The Russian Empire: A Multi-Ethnic History*. London: Longman.

Karcha, R. (1958). *'The Status of Popular Education in the Northern Caucasus'*. Caucasian Review: Munich, no. 7.

Kasumov, A. Kh. (1992). *Genotsid Adygov: Iz Istorii Bor'by Adygov za Nezavisimost' v XIX Veke*. Nalchik: LOGOS.

Katzenstein, Peter, ed. (1996). *The Culture of National Security: Norms and Identity in World Politics*. New York: Columbia University Press. (Online access: http://www.fb03.uni-frankfurt.de/45503391/Introduction-from-Katzenstein-1996---The-Culture-of-National-Security.pdf)

Kaya, A. (2004). *'Political Participation Strategies of the Circassian Diaspora in Turkey'*. Mediterranean Politics, 9 (2). (Online access: http://dx.doi.org/10.1080/1362939042000221286)

Kaya, A. (2014). *'The Circassian Diaspora In and Outside Turkey Construction of Transnational Space in the Post-Communist Era'*. Problems of Post-Communism, vol. 61, no. 4.

Kaya, Ayhan (2013). *Europeanization and Tolerance in Turkey: The Myth of Toleration*. London: Palgrave.

Keck, M. E., and K. Sikkink (1998). *Activists beyond Borders: Advocacy Networks in International Politics*. Ithaca, NY: Cornell University Press.

Kemper, Michael (2010). *Companjen, Françoise, ed. Exploring the Caucasus in the 21st Century: Essays on Culture, History and Politics in a Dynamic Context*. Amsterdam: Amsterdam University Press.

Khashig, Inal (2011). *The politics behind the Georgian parliament's recognition of the Circassian genocide*. 13 July. (Online Access: https://www.international-alert.org/blog/politics-behind-georgian-parliaments-recognition-circassian-genocide)

Khlynina, T.P. (2013). *'History, Politics and National Construction in the Northern Caucasus'*. (in Ukrainian). Historical and Political Science Studies: No. 4 (54).

Khodarkovsky, Michael (2008). *The north Caucasus during the Russian conquest; 1600-1850s*. University of Pittsburgh. (Online Access: https://www.ucis.pitt.edu/nceeer/2008_821-08g_Khodarkovsky.pdf)

Khoon, Yahya (2015). '*Prince of Circassia: Sefer Bey Zanuko and the Circassian Struggle for Independence*'. Journal of Caucasian Studies. 1 (1). (Online Access: http://dergipark.gov.tr/download/article-file/174064)

Khubiev-Karachaily, Islam (1922). '*Kabardino-Karachaevskii vopros*'. Zhizn' natsional'nostei 4 (133).

King, Charles (2007). '*Imagining Circassia: David Urquhart and the Making of North Caucasus Nationalism*'. The Russian Review, No.66. (Online access: http://www.circassianworld.com/new/general/1348-imagining-circassia-urquhart-by-king.html)

King, Charles (2008). The Ghost of Freedom: A History of the Caucasus. New York City, NY: Oxford University Press.

Kirişçi, Kemal (2000). '*Disaggregating Turkish Citizenship and Immigration Practices*'. Middle Eastern Studies 36 (3):1. (Online access: https://www.tandfonline.com/doi/abs/10.1080/00263200008701316)

Klaproth, Julius von (1814). *Travels in the Caucasus and Georgia, Performed in the Years 1807 and 1808*. London: Henry Colburn. Translated from the German by F. Shoberl. (Online access: http://data.cervantesvirtual.com/manifestation/257303?lang=en)

Kodzaev, A. (1903). *Drevnie Osetiny i Osetiia*. Vladikavkaz: Tipografiia R. Segal' i S-v'ia.

Kohl, P. & Trifonov, Viktor (2014). *The prehistory of the Caucasus: internal developments and external interactions*. (Online access: https://www.researchgate.net/publication/313508369_The_prehistory_of_the_Caucasus_internal_developments_and_external_interactions)

Kolossov, V. (1999). '*Ethnic and political identities and territorialities in the post-Soviet space*'. Geo Journal Vol. 48, No. 2.

Köremezli, Ibrahim (2004). *The Place of the Ottoman Empire in the Russo-Circassian War (1830-1864)*. Bilkent University Thesis. Bilkent University. (Online access: https://aheku.net/f1jok/files/3946/1-russo-circassian-war.pdf)

Kosven, M. O. (1961). *Ètnografiya i istoriya Kavkaza*, [Ethnography and History of the Caucasus], Moscow.

Krag, H. and Funch, L. (1995). *The North Caucasus: Minorities at a Crossroads*. Minority Rights Group International: London.

Kramer, Mark (2005a). '*The Perils of Counterinsurgency: Russia's War in Chechnya*'. International Security, 29/3.

Kramer, Mark (2005b). '*Guerilla Warfare, Counterinsurgency and Terrorism in the North Caucasus: The Military Dimension of the Russian-Chechen Conflict*'. Europe-Asia Studies: 57/2.

Kreiten, Irma (2009). '*A colonial experiment in cleansing: the Russian conquest of Western Caucasus, 1856–65*'. Journal of Genocide Research, 11(2-3), June–September.

Ksalova, Bella (2010). *Adyge Khasse: idea of united Circassia is no threat to Russia's integrity*. Caucasian Knot. (Online access: http://www.eng.kavkaz-uzel.eu/articles/12289)

Kuchukov, M.M. (1992). *Natsionalnoe samosoznanie i mezhnatsionalnye otnoshenia*. Nalchik.

Kuipers, A. H. (1960). *Phoneme and morpheme in Kabardian* (eastern Adyghe). The Hague: Mouton & Co.

Kukiel, M. (1955). *Czartoryski and European Unity 1770–1861*. New Jersey: Princeton.

Kumikov, Tugan Khabasovich (1994). *Vyselenie Adygov v Turtsiiu—Posledstvie Kavkazskoi Voiny*. Nalchik: T. Kh.

Kumykov, Tugan (2003). *Arkhivnye Materialy o Kavkazskoi Voinei Vyselenii Cherkesov (Adygov) v Turtsiiu*. Nalchik.

Kushabiyev, Anzor, Neflasheva, N., Topçu, M., and Orhan, O. (2012). '*Syrian Circassians*'. ORSAM Report No: 130, November.

Kusheva, E. (1963). '*Narody Severnogo Kavkaza i ikh sviazi s Rossiei: vtoraia polovina XVI-30-e gody XVII veka*'. Moscow: Izdatel'stvo Akademii Nauk.

Lanskoy, M. (2000). '*Who's afraid of Yusup Soslambekov*'. Central Asia – Caucasus Analyst article. (Online access: https://www.cacianalyst.org/publications/analytical-articles/item/7162-analytical-articles-caci-analyst-2000-9-27-art-7162.html)

Lanzillotti, I. T. (2016). '*Historiography and the politics of land, identity, and belonging in the twentieth-century North Caucasus*'. Nationalities Papers, 44:4.

Laruelle, M. (2017). *Kadyrovism: Hardline Islam as Tool of the Kremlin?*. Russia/NIS Center, Russie.Nei. Visions 99.

Latham, R. G. (1859). *Descriptive Ethnology*. London: J. Van Voorst. (Online access: https://archive.org/details/descriptiveethn00lathgoog)

Latham, R. G. (1862). *Elements of Comparative Philology*. London: Walton and Maberly. (Online access: https://catalog.hathitrust.org/Record/008674441)

Latka, Jerzy S. (1992). *Lehistan'dan Gelen Sefirler: Türkiye-Polonya İlişkilerinin Altı Yüzyılı*. translated by Antoni and Nalan Sarkady, İstanbul.

Lavie, Smadar and Swedenburg, Ted, eds. (1996). *Displacement, Diaspora and Geographies of Identity*. USA: Duke University Press

Lavrov, L. I. (1956). *Proizkhozhdenie Kabardintsev i zaselenie imi nineshnei territorii*. [The Origin of the Kabardians and Their Settlement in Their Present Territory]. Sovetskaya ètnografiya, No.1.

Leitzinger, Antero (2004). *The Circassian Genocide*. Global Politician. (Online access: https://web.archive.org/web/20131109084500/http://www.globalpolitician.com/default.asp?2243-circassia)

Lepretre, M. (2002). *Language Policies in the Soviet Successor States: A Brief Assessment on Language Linguistic Rights and National Identity*. (Online access: http://www.ucm.es/BUCM/cee/papeles/03/03.PDF)

Leprêtre, Marc (2002). *Language Policy in the Russian Federation: language diversity and national identity*. Noves SL: Revista de Sociolingüística internacional, Primavera. (Online access: http://www.gencat.cat/llengua/noves)

Levene, Mark (2005). *Genocide in the Age of the Nation State*. London; New York: I.B. Tauris, Levene.

Lewak, Adam (1935). *Dzieje Emigracji Polskiej w Turcji, 1831-1878*. Warszawa: Nak. Instytutu Wschodniego.

Lewis, Martin W. (2012). *The Circassian Mystique and Its Historical Roots Submitted*. (Online access: http://www.geocurrents.info/place/russia-ukraine-and-caucasus/the-circassian-mystique-and-its-historical-roots#ixzz57qkX9l2r)

Libedinsky, Y. (1951). *Narti: Kabardinskièpos*. [The Narts: A Kabardian Epos] Moscow: Academy of Sciences of the USSR

Libedinsky, Yuri (1951). *Narti: Kabardinski èpos*. [The Narts: A Kabardian Epos] Moscow: Academy of Sciences of the USSR.

Littleton, C. S. (1979). '*The Holy Grail, the Cauldron of Annwn, and the Narty-Amonga, a Further Note on the Sarmatian Connection*'. Journal of American Folklore, no. 92.

Littleton, C. S. and Thomas, A. C., '*The Sarmatian Connection: New Light on the Origin of the Arthurian and Holy Grail Legends*'. Journal of American Folklore, 91, 1978, pp 513-27.

Loewe, Louis (1854). *A Dictionary of the Circassian Language: in Two Parts: English-Circassian -Turkish, and Circassian-English-Turkish*. London: Bell. (Online Access: https://books.google.pl/books/about/A_dictionary_of_the_Circassian_language.html?id=0400AQAAIAAJ&redir_esc=y)

Luxenburg, Norman (1998). *Rusların Kafkasya'yı İşgalinde İngiliz Politikası ve İmam Şamil*. translated by Sedat Özden, İstanbul.

Makarov, D. and Mukhametshin, R. (2003). *Official and unofficial Islam*. eds H. Pilkington and G. Yemelianova, Islam in Post-Soviet Russia: Public and Private Faces. Routledge Curzon: London.

Malkki, Liisa (2001). *National Geographic: The Rooting of Peoples and the Territorialization of National Identity among Scholars and Refugees*. In A. Gupta and J. Ferguson, eds. Culture, Power, Place: Explorations in Critical Anthropology. Duke University Press.

Mango, Andrew (1999). Atatürk. London: John Murray.

Marcus, J. (2018). *Russia v the West: Is this a new Cold War?* BBC: 1 April.(Online access: https://www.bbc.com/news/world-europe-43581449)

Markedonov, S. (2011). *Kavkazkaya proektsiya vlastnoi rokirovki v Rossii* [Caucasian projection of castling power in Russia]. Polit. (Online Access: http://polit.ru/article/2011/09/30/Caucas)

Markedonov, S. (2015). *'Islamskoegosudarvstvo: Ugroza dlia bolshogo Kavkaza'*. Russian International Affairs Council, 9 November. (Online Access: http://russiancouncil.ru/analytics-and-comments/analytics/islamskoe-gosudarstvo-ugroza-dlya-bolshogo-kavkaza/?sphrase_id=1833977)

Markovits, A. and Rensmann, L. (2010). *Gaming the World: How Sports Are Reshaping Global Politics and Culture*. Princeton: Princeton University Press

Markwick, R. D. (2006). *'Cultural History under Khrushchev and Brezhnev: from Social Psychology to Mentalités'*. The Russian Review, N.65.

Marshall, Alex (2010). *The Caucasus Under Soviet Rule - North Caucasian Soviet Republic*. New York City: Routledge.

McGregor, Andrew James (2006). *A Military History of Modern Egypt: From the Ottoman Conquest to the Ramadan War*. Greenwood Publishing Group.

Melvin, N. J. (2007). *Building Stability in the North Caucasus Ways Forward for Russia and the European Union*. SIPRI Policy Paper No. 16, Stockholm International Peace Research Institute.

Meyer, James H. (2007). *'Immigration, Return, and the Politics of Citizenship: Russian Muslims in the Ottoman Empire, 1880–1914'*. International Journal of Middle East Studies 39 (1): 16. (Online access: http://jhmeyer.net/Meyer-IJMES%20Article.pdf)

Meyer, James H. (2007). *'Immigration, Return, and the Politics of Citizenship: Russian Muslims in the Ottoman Empire, 1880–1914'*. International Journal of Middle East Studies; 39 (1).

Mikaberidze, Alexander (2005). *The Russian officer Corps in the Revolutionary and Napoleonic wars 1792-1815*. Savas Beatie, New York.

Miller, David (1995). *On Nationality*. London: Oxford University Press.

Minahan, James (2000). *One Europe, Many Nations: a Historical Dictionary of European National Groups*. Westport, USA: Greenwood.

Minahan, James (2000). *One Europe, Many Nations: a Historical Dictionary of European National Groups*. Westport, USA: Greenwood.

Minorsky, V. (1943). *Tadhkirat al-mulūk: A Manual of Safavid Administration* (circa 1137/1725). Persian text in facsimile. London, Luzac. MNK Czartoryskich Ew. 1257; Muzeum Narodowe w Krakowie Biblioteka.

Motyl, A. J. (1990). *Sovietology, Rationality, Nationality*. Coming to Grips with Nationalism in the USSR. New York: Columbia University Press.

Mozzhukhin, A. (2015). *Traditsionnogo Islamana Severnom Kavkaze net*. Lenta.ru, 4 March. (Online Access: https://lenta.ru/articles/2015/03/04/salafism)

Mullen, Christopher A.; Ryan, J. Atticus (1998). *Unrepresented Nations and Peoples Organization*. The Hague: Kluwer Law International.

Müller, M. (2011). *State dirigisme in megaprojects: governing the 2014 Winter Olympics in Sochi*. Environment and Planning A 43.

Müller, M. (2013). *Sochi and the 2014 Olympics: Game over*. Center for Governance and Culture in Europe University of St.Gallen.

Müller, Martin (2013). '*Sochi and the 2014 Olympics: Game over*'. Online Journal of the Center for Governance and Culture in Europe University of St. Gallen. Euxeinos 12. (Online Access: https://serval.unil.ch/resource/serval:BIB_B2959275F30D.P001/REF)

Murinson, A. (2006). '*The strategic depth doctrine of Turkish foreign policy*'. Middle Eastern Studies, 42:6.

Murray, C. A. (2002). '*The Third Sector: Cultural Diversity and Civil Society*'. Canadian Journal of Communication 27 (2).

Nahaylo, B. and Swoboda, V. (1990). *Soviet Disunion*. A History of the Nationalities Problem in the USSR. London: Hamish Hamilton.

Namitok A. (1956). '*The Voluntary Adherence of Kabarda (Eastern Circassia) to Russia*'. Caucasian Review, Munich (CRM), No. 2.

Namrouqa, Hana (2010). *New academy to promote Circassian language, traditions*. The Amman Times.

Narochnitskii, A. L. (ed.) (1988). *Istoriia Narodov Severnogo Kavkaza* (Konets XVIII v.-1917 g.). Moscow: Nauka.

Natho, Kadir I. (2009). *Circassian History*. Xlibris Corporation. (Online access: https://books.google.pl/books/about/Circassian_History.html?id=eE2pDLgibVoC&redir_esc=y)

Natho, Kadir I. (2010). *Memoirs*. Xlibris Corporation. (Online access: https://books.google.pl/books/about/Memoirs.html?id=1OdMngEACAAJ&redir_esc=y)

Nevskaia, V. (1967). *Ocherki istorii Karachaevo-Cherkesii*. Stavropol': Stavropol'skoe Knizhnoe Izdatel'stvo.

Nichols, J. (1986). *Head-Marking and Dependent-Marking Grammar. Language.* Linguistic Society of America. 62 (1).

Nieto, W. A. S. (2011). '*The Olympic Challenge: Russia's Strategy for the Establishment of Security in the North Caucasus before 2014*'. Journal of Slavic Military Studies, Taylor & Francis Group.

Nolde, B., (1952– 1953). '*La Formation de l'Empire russe, Paris: Institut d'Etudes Slaves*'. Volumes 2, and Kappeler, A., The Russian Empire: to the 1850s. (Online access: http://www.circassianworld.com/Hewitt_Kymenlaakso. pdf)

OC Media (2017). *South Ossetia to be renamed 'Alania' as Bibilov wins presidential election*. OC Media: 10 April. (Online Access: http://oc-media.org/south-ossetia-to-be-renamed-alania-as-bibilov-wins-presidential-election/)

Ogurtsov, A. (1989). *Подавление философии* [Suppression of philosophy]. Суровая драма народа: Учёные и публицисты о природе сталинизма [The harsh drama of the people: Scientists and publicists about the nature of Stalinism] (in Russian). Moscow: Politizdat.

Oppong, Steward Harrison (2013). *'Religion and Identity'*. American International Journal of Contemporary Research Vol. 3 No. 6; June. (Online Access: http://www.aijcrnet.com/journals/Vol_3_No_6_June_2013/2.pdf)

ORSAM (2012). *Syrian Circassians*. Center for Middle Eastern Strategic Studies (Ortadogu Stratejic Arastirmalar Merkezi - ORSAM), Report No: 130. (Online Access: http://www.croworld.org/wp-content/uploads/2014/05/Syrian-Circassians.pdf)

Oskanian, K. (2011). *Turkey's global strategy: Turkey and the Caucasus*. IDEAS reports - special reports, Kitchen, Nicholas (ed.) LSE IDEAS, London School of Economics and Political Science, London, UK.

Özgür, E. (2011). *'The North Caucasian and Abkhaz Diasporas; Their Lobbying Activities in Turkey'*. In Caucasus Studies: Migration, Society and Language, Caucasus Studies 4, edited by Karina Vamling.

Pain, E. (2009). *'Current Russian policy in the north Caucasus'*. North Caucasus Weekly Volume: 5 Issue: 45. (Online Access: https://jamestown.org/program/current-russian-policy-in-the-north-caucasus-2/)

Pattie, S. (2005). *New Homeland for an Old Diaspora*. In: Levy, A. & Weingrod, A. (eds.). Homelands and Diasporas: Holy Lands and Other Places, Stanford, California: Stanford University Press.

Persson, E. (2013). *Olympism and Empire: The Olympic Myth in the Contestation of the Caucasus*. In The Sochi Predicament: Contexts, Characteristics and Challenges of the Olympic Winter Games 2014, edited by B. Petersson and K. Vamling. Newcastle upon Tyne: Cambridge Scholars.

Petersen, Leif Inge Ree (2013). *Siege Warfare and Military Organization in the Successor States* (400-800 AD).

Petersson Bo, & K. Vamling (2013). *The Sochi Predicament. Contexts, Challenges and Characteristics of the Olympic Winter Games in 2014*. Newcastle: Cambridge Scholars Publishing. (Online access: http://militarylegitimacyreview.com/wp-content/uploads/2014/01/The-Sochi-Predicament-Sample.pdf)

Petersson, B. and Vamling, K. (2013). *'Display Window or Tripwire? The Sochi Winter Games, the Russian Great Power Ideal and the Legitimacy of Vladimir Putin'*. Euxeinos, No. 12.(Online Access: https://gce.unisg.ch/-/media/dateien/instituteundcenters/gce/euxeinos/petersson-vamling-euxeinos-12_2013.pdf?la=en&hash=398E8184BA9E268F5FCFE85D5EE7BC5169F684CB)

Petersson, B. and Vamling, K. (2017). *'Fifteen minutes of fame long gone: Circassian activism before and after the Sochi Olympics'*. Sport in Society: 20/4.

Pirani, S. (2010). *Change in Putin's Russia: Power, Money and People*. New York: Pluto Press.

Polandov, D. (2010). Virtual Circassia. Prague Watchdog. (Online access: http://www.watchdog.cz/?top_from=36&lang=1)

Polat, H. B. (2008). *Conference Presentation on the Role of the ICA*. William Paterson University, New Jersey.

Połczyński, Michael (2014). *Eagles in the Caucasus: polish-circassian cooperation against Russia in the 19th century*. CircassianWorld. (Online access: http://www.circassianworld.com/history/war-and-exile/1615-eagles-in-the-caucasus-polish-circassian-cooperation-against-russia-in-the-19th-century)

Polovinkina (1999). *Cherkesiia—Bol' Moia. Istoricheskii Ocherk*. (drevneishee vremia—nachalo XX v.). Maykop: RIPO.

Polovinkina, T. V. (1999). *Cherkesiia – bol moia*. Maykop.

Popov, Maxim (2017). *'Resolving Identity-based Conflicts in the North Caucasus'*. Periodica Polytechnica Social and Management Sciences: 25(1). (Online access: https://pp.bme.hu/so/article/view/9535)

Prymak, Homas M. (1982). *'The Strange Life of Sadyk Pasha'*. Forum: A Ukrainian Review, No. 50.

Qaghirmes, B. (1992) *'ЕЩТАУЭМРЭ ЩТАУЧЫМРЭ*. Yeschtawemre Schtawichimre [... and Flint]', in Іуащхьэмахуэ. Waschhemaxwe, no. 4.

Rahman, M. S. (2009). *'Georgia and Russia: What Caused the August War'*. Identity, Culture & Politics: An Afro-Asian Dialogue. 10 (1).

Rannut, U. (2011) *Maintenance of the Circassian Language in Jordan Self-identification, attitudes, policies and practices as indicators of linguistic vitality*. Amman: IRI Publications.

Richmond, W. (2013). *The Circassian Genocide* (Genocide, Political Violence, Human Right). Rutgers University Press;

Richmond, Walter (2008). *The Northwest Caucasus: Past, Present, Future*. Central Asian Studies Series; Routledge. (Online Access: https://books.google.pl/books/about/The_Northwest_Caucasus.html?id=sYnYmAEACAAJ&redir_esc=y)

Richmond, Walter (2013). *The Circassian Genocide*. Rutgers University Press (Online access: https://books.google.com/books/about/The_Circassian_Genocide.html?id=LHlwZwpA70cC)

Rjabchikov, Sergei V. (1999). *The Scythians, Sarmatians, Meotians, Russians and Circassians: Interpretation of the Ancient Cultures*. The Slavonic Antiquity. (Online Access: http://public.kubsu.ru/~usr02898/sl2.htm)

Ro'i, Y. (2000). *Islam in the Soviet Union: From World War II to Perestroika*. Columbia University Press: New York, N.Y.

Robarts, Andrew (2008). *Treaty of Bucharest*. In Ágoston, Gábor; Masters, Bruce. Encyclopedia of the Ottoman Empire.

Roudik, P. (2008). *Russian Federation: Legal Aspects of War in Georgia*. Library of Congress. (Online Access: https://www.loc.gov/law/help/legal-aspects-of-war/russian-georgia-war.php)

Rouse, R. (1991). *'Mexican Migration and the Social Space of Postmodernism'*. Diaspora 1(1).

Roy, A. (2008). *'Russia resurgent? Moscow's campaign to coerce Georgia to peace'*. International Affairs. 84 (6).

Royle, Trevor (2000). *'Crimea: The Great Crimean War, 1854–1856'*. Palgrave Macmillan.

Rudnytsky, Ivan L. (1987). *Michal Czajkowski's Cossack Project during the Crimean War: An Analysis of Ideas*. Essays in Modern Ukrainian History, edited by Peter L.Rudnytsky, Edmonton.

Russia Today (2009). *Chechen self-proclaimed government-in-exile lays down weapons*. 29 July. (Online Access: https://russian.rt.com/Top_News/2009-07-27/chechen-self-proclaimed-government-in-exile-lays-down-weapons.html)

Sakwa, R. (2012). *'Russia: from Stalemate to Crisis'*. The Brown Journal of World Affairs 19:1.

Saray, Mehmet (ed.) (1988). *Kafkas Araştırmaları I*. Istanbul: Acar Yayınları.

Schroeder, Paul W. (1994). *The Transformation of European Politics 1763–1848*. New York: Oxford University Press.

Shakhnazarian, N. (2008). *Adyghi Krasnodarskogo kraia*. Krasnodar.

Shamba, S. (2008). *Сергей Шамба о 20-летии движения "Аидгылара" и национально-освободительной борьбе народа Абхазии*. REGNUM News Agency. Retrieved 31 January 2013.

Shami, Seteney (1998). *'Circassian Encounters: The Self as Other and the Production of the Homeland in the North Caucasus'*. Development and Change, No. 29 (4). (Online access: http://www.circassianworld.com/analysis/1205-circassianencounters-shami)

Shami, Seteney (2000). *'Prehistories of Globalization: Circassian Identity in Motion'*. Public Culture, Vol.12, Issue 1, Winter, Editors Arjun Appadurai, Duke university press. (Online access: https://doi.org/10.1215/08992363-12-1-177 pp. 178-181)

Shami, Seteney (2009). *'Historical Process of Identity Formation: Displacement, Settlement, and Self - Representations of the Circassians in Jordan'*. Iran and the Caucasus, Vol. 13, Brill.

Sheffer, G. (2003). *Diaspora Politics*. New York: Cambridge University Press.

Shenfield, Stephen D. (1999). *The Circassians: a forgotten genocide*. In Levene, Mark and Penny Roberts, eds., The massacre in history. Oxford and New York: Berghahn Books. Series: War and Genocide; 1.

Sherr, J. (2017). *Nagorno-Karabakh between Old and New Geopolitics*. Cornell, Svante E. (ed.) The International Politics of the Armenian-Azerbaijani Conflict: The Original "Frozen Conflict" & European Security, New York: Palgrave Macmillan.

Shevtsova, L. (2012). *'Russia under Putin: Titanic looking for its iceberg'*. Communist and Post-Communist Studies: 45.

Shmulevich, A. (2015). *Cherkesskiyvopros* [Circassian Question]. (Online Access: http://www.mesoeurasia.org/archives/120)

Shnirelman, V. (2006). *Быть Аланами. Интеллектуалы и по- литика на Северном Кавказе в XX веке* [Being Alans. Intellectuals and politics in the North Caucasus in the 20th century]. Moscow.

Sicker, Martin (2001). *The Islamic World in Decline: From the Treaty of Karlowitz to the Disintegration of the Ottoman Empire*. Praeger Publishers.

Skochen, Stefaniia (1998). *Yüzyıldaki Polonya-Kuzey Kafkasya İlişkileri*. Tarih ve Toplum, Vol. 29, No. 174.

Smeets, H. J. (1984). *Studies in West Circassian phonology and morphology*. Leiden: The Hakuchi Press.

Smirnov, A. (2006). *'Disputable anniversary could provoke new crisis in Adygeya'*. Jamestown Foundation's Eurasia Daily Monitor Volume 3, Number 168, September 13. (Online Access: https://jamestown.org/program/disputable-anniversary-could-provoke-new-crisis-in-adygeya/#.U4VKCy9Vt7w)

Smirnova, A.S. (1993). *Karachayevo-Cherkesiya: etnopoliticheskaya i etnokul'turnaya situatsiya*. Moscow, Rossiiskaya Akademiya Nauk, Institut Etnologii i Antropologii.

Smith, Anthony D. (1981). *The Ethnic Revival in the Modern World*. Cambridge University Press.

Smith, M. P., and Guarnizo, L. E., eds. (1998). *Transnationalism from Below: Comparative Urban and Community Research*. New Brunswick, NJ: Transaction.

Sochi (2014). *Administrativno-territorial'noye ustroystvo Sochi*. 1866-1945. [Administrative and territorial structure of Sochi]. sochi.com. Archived from the original on February 21, 2014. (Online access: https://sochi.com/article-of-sochi/6148/337388/)

Şoenu, M. F. (1993). *Çerkes Meselesi*. Bedir Yayınları: Istanbul.

Souleimanov, E. (2005). *'Chechnya, Wahhabism and the invasion of Dagestan'*. Middle East Review of International Affairs, vol. 9, no. 4. (Online Access: http://meria.idc.ac.il/journal/2005/issue4/jvol9 no4in.html)

Spencer, Edmund (1838). *Travels in the Western Caucasus, including a Tour through Imeritia, Mingrelia, Turkey, Moldavia, Galicia, Silesia, and Moravia in 1836*. London: H. Colburn.

Stalin, J. and others (1938). *Short Course History of the Soviet Communist Party*. Moscow.

Stone, David R. (2006). *A Military History of Russia: From Ivan the Terrible to the War in Chechnya*. Greenwood Publishing Group.

Szporluk, Roman (1994). *National Identity and Ethnicity in Russia and the new States of Eurasia*. M.E.Sharpe, New York.

Taitbout, De Marigny (1837). *Three Voyages in the Black Sea to the Coast of Circassia*. London, J. Murray. (Online Access: http://onlinebooks.library.upenn.edu/webbin/book/lookupid?key=olbp56395)

Tarran, Michel (1991). 'The Orthodox Mission in the North Caucasus - End of the 18th, beginning of the 19th Century'. Central Asian Survey, Vol. 10/1-2. (Online access: http://www.tandfonline.com/doi/abs/10.1080/02634939108400738)

Taylor, Charles (1989). *The Sources of the Self: The Making of the Modern Identity.* Cambridge, MA: Harvard University Press.

Temizkan, A. (2009). *'Yüzyılda Çarlık Rusya'sının Kafkas Ordusu'nda Lehistanlılar'.* Karadeniz Araştırmaları, 20. Kış.

Temizkan, A. (2010). *'Lehistanlılarin İstanbul'da lobi faaliyetleri ve Kafkasya'ya lejyon gönderme girişimleri'.* Türklük Bilimi Araştırmaları Dergisi, 28.

Temperley, Harold (1964). *England and the Near East; The Crimea.* London.

The Caucasus Trust (CT) and the Federation of the Caucasus Associations (KAFFED) (2005). *The two of the most prominent Caucasian organizations in Turkey, give the figure of seven million for the number of people in Turkey with Caucasian ancestry with the majority of them being Circassian* (Caucasus Trust, n.d.). A prominent researcher speaks of two to three million Circassians (Papsu), Nart Ajans: http://www.nartajans.net/site/haberler_5573_turkiye_deki_cerkes_koyleri.html.)

Tillett, L. (1969). *The Great Friendship: Soviet Historians on the Non-Russian Nationalities.* Chapel Hill: University of North Carolina Press.

Tishkov, V. (1996). *Ethnicity, Nationalism and Conflict in and after the Soviet Union: The Mind of Aflame.* London: United Nations Research Institute for Social Development.

Tlisova, F. (2010). *'Hidden Nations, Enduring Crimes conference'.* Eurasia Daily Monitor 7 (58).

Tlisova, Fatima (2009). *'Support for Circassian Nationalism Grows in the North* Caucasus'. Georgiandaily.net, through Adyga NatPress. (Online access: http://www.natpress.net/index.php?newsid=3931)

Tlisova, Fatima (2009). *'Youth Activists Unravel Kremlin Status-Quo in the Circassian Heartland: The Wind of Freedom is approaching'.* The Jamestown Foundation: North Caucasus Weekly Volume: 10 Issue: 15. (Online access: https://jamestown.org/program/youth-activists-unravel-kremlin-status-quo-in-the-circassian-heartland-the-wind-of-freedom-is-approaching/)

Tokluoglu, Ceylan (2005). *'Definitions of national identity, nationalism and ethnicity in post-Soviet Azerbaijan in the 1990s'.* Ethnic and Racial Studies. Volume 28 - Issue 4. (Online access: https://www.tandfonline.com/doi/abs/10.1080/01419870500092951)

Tölölyan, K. (2003). *The American model of diasporic discourse.* Diasporas and Ethnic Migrants: Germany, Israel, and Post-Soviet Successor States in Comparative Perspective, London: Frank Cass Publishers.

Toumarkine, Alexandre (2000). *Balkan and Caucasian Immigrant Associations: Community and Politics.* In S. Yerasimos, G. Seufert, and K. Vorhoff, eds. Civil Society in the Grip of Nationalism: Studies on Political Culture in Contemporary Turkey. Würzburg, Germany: Ergon Verlag.

Trakho, R. (1992). *Cherkesy.* Nalchik, 1992.

Trenin, D. V. and Malashenko, A. V. (2004). *Russia's Restless Frontier: The Chechnya Factor in Post- Soviet Russia.* Carnegie Foundation for International Peace: Washington, DC.

Tsibenko, Veronika V. & Tsibenko, Sergey N. (2015). *Circassian Question: Transformation of Content and Perception.* Bylye Gody, Sochi State University: Vol. 36, Is. 02. (Online access: http://bg.sutr.ru/journals_n/1433510573.pdf)

Tsibenko, Veronika Vitalyevna (2015). *'The War of Conferences in Russia and Turkey: The Circassian Dimension'.* Asian Social Science; Vol. 11, No. 14. (Online Access: http://www.ccsenet.org/journal/index.php/ass/article/view/49106)

Tucker, Spencer C. (ed.) (2010). *Overview of 1800-1850: Chronology.* A Global Chronology of Conflict: From the Ancient World to the Modern Middle East. ABC-CLIO.

Tuna, Fikri (2004). *Diyane: Çerkes Kadınları Yardımlaşma Derneği'nin Düşünce Yayınıdır.* Istanbul: Asyayın.

Tunaya, Tarık Zafer (1952). *Şark-ı Karib Çerkesleri Temin-i Hukuk Cemiyeti.* Türkiye'de Siyasi Partiler Cilt II. Doğan Kardeş Yayınları: İstanbul.

Turan, M. Aydın (1998). *Osmanlı Dönemi Kuzey Kafkasya Diasporası Tarihinden Şimali Kafkas Cemiyeti.* Tarih ve Toplum: 172.

Urushadze, Levan Z. (2005). *About the history of the question of unity of the Caucasian Peoples.* J. Amirani, XIII, Montreal-Tbilisi.

Usmanov, Lyoma (1999). *The Chechen Nation: A Portrait of Ethnical Features.* Washington, D.C.

Van Bruinessen, Maarten Martinus (1978). *Agha, Shaikh and State: On the Social and Political Organization of Kurdistan.* Utrecht: University of Utrecht (London: Zed Books, 1992). (Online access: https://libcom.org/files/van%20Bruinessen,%20Martin%20[1992]%20Agha,%20Shaikh%20and%20State%20-%20The%20Social%20and%20Political%20Structures%20of%20Kurdistan.pdf)

Vardania, G. (2007). *'Episodes from the Past of the Caucasian Diaspora (Abkhaz and Adyghe)'* [in Russian]. Kavkaziglobalizatsia [Caucasus and Globalization], 1 (2).

Vasmer, Max (1953–1958). *Russisches etymologisches Wörterbuch.* Heidelberg: Winter

Ware, R. B. and Kisriev, E. (2002). *'Prospects for Political Stability and Economic Development in Dagestan'.* Central Asian Survey: 21/2.

Weeks, Theodore R. (2004). *'Russification: Word and Practice 1863–1914'.* Proceedings of the American Philosophical Society. 148 (4) (Online access: https://web.archive.org/web/20120523232533/http://www.amphilsoc.org/sites/default/files/480407.pdf)

Winrow, G. (2009). *'Turkey, Russia and the Caucasus: Common and Diverging Interests'.* Russia and Eurasia Programme/Europe Programme: November.

Wood, Tony (2007). *Chechnya: the Case for Independence.* Verso.

Yeğen, Mesut (2004). '*Citizenship and Ethnicity in Turkey*'. Middle Eastern Studies 40, no.6. (Online access: https://ais.ku.edu.tr/course/20203/yegen-citizenship-ethnicity.pdf)

Yemelianova, Galina (2014). *Islam nationalism and state in the Muslim Caucasus.*

Young, Iris Marion (1990). *Justice and the Politics of Difference.* Princeton, N.J.: Princeton University Press. (Online Access: https://books.google.pl/books/about/Justice_and_the_Politics_of_Difference.html?id=Q6keKguPrsAC&redir_esc=y)

Zhemukhov, S. (2010). '*Ponars*'. Eurasia Policy Memo 118.

Zhemukhov, S. (2010). '*Russia and Georgia: the Circassian question*'. Open Democracy, 9 November. (Online Access: https://www.opendemocracy.net/od-russia/sufian-zhemukhov/russia-and-georgia-circassian-question)

Zhemukhov, S. (2012). '*The Birth of Modern Circassian Nationalism*'. Nationalities Papers 40 (4): Taylor & Francis Online

Zhemukhov, Sufian & King, Charles (2013). '*Dancing the Nation in the North Caucasus*'. Slavic Review, Vol. 72, No. 2. (Online Access: http://www.jstor.org/stable/10.5612/slavicreview.72.2.0287)

Zhemukhov, Sufian (2009). '*The Circassian Dimension of the 2014 Sochi Olympics*'. PONARS Policy Memo, No. 65 - Georgetown University. (Online access: https://web.archive.org/web/20091011120907/http://www.circassianworld.com/new/general/1382-circassian-dimension-2014sochi-szhemukh.html)

Zhemukhov, Sufian (2012). '*The birth of modern Circassian nationalism*'. Nationalities Papers Vol. 40, No. 4, July. (Online access: https://www.tandfonline.com/doi/abs/10.1080/00905992.2012.674019)

Zuckerman, Constantine (2007). '*The Khazars and Byzantium –The First Encounter*'. In Golden, Peter B.; Ben-Shammai, Haggai; Róna-Tas, András. The World of the Khazars: New Perspectives. Handbuch der Orientalistik: Handbook of Uralic studies. 17.

Zurcher, Erik J. (1993). *Turkey: A Modern History.* London: I.B. Taurus & Co Ltd.

www.ingramcontent.com/pod-product-compliance
Lightning Source LLC
Chambersburg PA
CBHW061419300426
44114CB00015B/1995